I0817515

NORTH AMERICAN
FIELD GUIDES

DECIDUOUS TREES

Samantha S. Bell

An Imprint of Abdo Reference | abdobooks.com

CONTENTS

WHAT ARE DECIDUOUS TREES?

Deciduous trees are trees that lose their leaves every year. They are also called broadleaf trees. This is because most deciduous trees have wide, flat leaves. Their shape helps the leaves capture a lot of sunlight.

Trees use sunlight to make their own food. They do this through a process called photosynthesis. The leaves contain a chemical called chlorophyll. It gives the leaves their green color. Chlorophyll absorbs sunlight. Trees use energy from sunlight to turn water and carbon dioxide into oxygen and a type of sugar called glucose. The trees use glucose to grow.

In fall, the days become shorter. There is not enough sunlight for deciduous trees to continue making glucose using photosynthesis. The chlorophyll in the leaves breaks down. The leaves lose their green color, allowing other colors to be seen. The leaves may turn red, yellow, orange, purple, or brown. Eventually the leaves fall from the tree. There are no more leaves for the tree to nourish. This helps the tree survive winter. New leaves will grow again in spring.

THE BENEFITS OF DECIDUOUS TREES

Trees help keep other living things healthy. During photosynthesis, trees absorb carbon dioxide from the atmosphere. In the process, they release oxygen that people and animals breathe. Trees also provide habitats and food for many birds and other animals.

Deciduous trees offer an extra benefit. When the leaves fall, they become leaf litter. Living things such as fungi, algae, insects, and earthworms on the ground break down the leaf litter. Fallen leaves provide nutrients to the soil. Leaf litter also helps insulate soil, keeping soil temperatures

from changing dramatically. Fallen leaves also reduce the amount of moisture that evaporates into the air, regulating soil moisture.

IDENTIFYING DECIDUOUS TREES

All deciduous trees lose their leaves. But the trees do not all look the same. People can look for certain traits to figure out the type of deciduous tree they see. For example, they can estimate the height of the tree and find out which trees grow that tall. People can examine the shape, color, texture, and arrangement of leaves. Some trees have compound leaves, meaning that each leaf is made up of multiple leaflets. Seeds, nuts, and fruits on a tree or on the ground nearby can also be signs of a tree's species. Many trees grow only in certain areas of the world and in specific habitats. People can use the location of a tree to identify it by researching species' ranges and habitats, which show where those species usually grow.

HOW TO USE THIS BOOK

Tab shows the tree category.

This paragraph gives information about the tree.

WILLOW FAMILY

BLACK WILLOW *(SALIX NIGRA)*

The black willow tree is native to the United States. It is a
...growing tree. Several trunks will often grow at different
...'s bark is dark brown to black with
...y scales. Male and female flowers
... Fruits grow on the female trees
...uit capsules open to release seeds.
...nd and water catch the long, silky
hairs and carry away the seeds. The leaves turn yellowish green in fall.

The tree's common name appears here.

HOW TO SPOT

Height: 30 to 140 feet (9 to 43 m)

Leaves: Green; up to 6 inches (15 cm) long; narrow with small teeth along the edges

Seeds: Hanging clusters of dry light brown capsules hold tiny green seeds attached to silky hairs

North American Range: Eastern United States and parts of Canada and Mexico

Habitat: Moist to wet soils such as floodplains, riverbanks, swamps, and marshes

How to Spot boxes give information about the tree's size, leaves, seeds, range, and habitat.

NATURAL MEDICINE

Willow trees have been used for healing purposes for centuries. The ancient Greeks used willow bark to make tea to treat stiff joints. Willow bark has also been used to reduce fevers. Some people still use willow bark instead of aspirin to relie...

Sidebars provide additional information about the topic.

The tree's scientific name appears here.

ASTERN COTTONWO

)PULUS DELTOIDES)

e eastern cottonwood is a large, fast-growing tree. me trees may grow more than six feet (1.8 m) each year. e tree has a large trunk that often splits into thick, urdy branches. The branches grow upright and droop at e tips. Flowers grow in clusters. They do not have petals id may be red, gold, or green. The tree's leaves turn yellow fall. In the late spring and early summer, its seed capsules pen. The seeds appear as cotton-like clusters.

Fun Facts give interesting information about the tree.

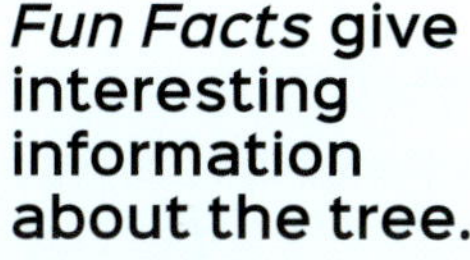

FUN FACT

Cottonwood trees are the fastest-growing native trees in North America.

HOW TO SPOT

Height: 75 to 100 feet (23 to 30 m)

Leaves: Smooth, glossy, paper-like leaves 3 to 6 inches (8 to 15 cm) long; light to medium green; triangular with curved teeth

Seeds: Green egg-shaped capsules containing many seeds with silky white hairs

North American Range: Southern Canada; southwestern, central, and eastern United States; and northern Mexico

Habitat: Along streams, riverbanks, and bottomlands

Seeds

Images show the tree.

83

LEGUME FAMILY

AMERICAN YELLOWWOOD

(CLADRASTIS KENTUKEA)

The American yellowwood gets its name from the yellow color of its wood. It is also known for its fragrant white flowers. Each flower is about one inch (2.5 cm) long. Large, drooping clusters of flowers hang from the tree's branches. The number of flowers that bloom alternates from year to year. One year the tree will be covered with flowers. The next year there will be far fewer. In fall the tree's leaves turn yellowish orange.

HOW TO SPOT

Height: 30 to 50 feet (9 to 15 m)

Leaves: 8 to 12 inches (20 to 30 cm) long; compound leaves of 7 to 9 leaflets

Seeds: Flat, brown seed pods; 2.5 to 4 inches (6 to 10 cm) long; contain 4 to 6 seeds

North American Range: Southeastern United States

Habitat: River valleys and moist, well-drained soils on slopes and ridges

HIS AND HERS FLOWERS

Trees may have male or female flowers or both. Male flowers produce pollen. When female flowers are pollinated, they produce fruits and seeds. Sometimes male and female flowers grow on different trees. Sometimes they grow on the same tree. Some trees have the male and female parts within the same flower.

BLACK LOCUST

(ROBINIA PSEUDOACACIA)

The black locust tree has a pair of sharp spines on each leaf. White flowers appear in May and June. Each flower has a yellow spot on the upper petal. The flowers bloom in clusters. These flowers are an important source of pollen and nectar for honeybees. However, the seeds, leaves, stem, and bark are poisonous. They are especially harmful to livestock such as horses and cattle.

HOW TO SPOT

Height: 40 to 70 feet (12 to 21 m)

Leaves: Bluish-green leaves 6 to 14 inches (15 to 36 cm) long; made up of oval leaflets

Seeds: Smooth, flat, dark fruit pods 2 to 4 inches (5 to 10 cm) long; contain 4 to 8 seeds

North American Range: From Pennsylvania through the Appalachian Mountains to northern Georgia and westward to Oklahoma

Habitat: Moist or wet forests, wooded slopes, roadsides, and old pastures

BLUE PALO VERDE

(PARKINSONIA FLORIDA)

The blue palo verde is a small tree with a crooked trunk and many thin, zigzagging branches. Small, straight spines grow near some new leaves, but they are not sharp. The blue palo verde does not have leaves for most of the year. It drops leaves in response to weather conditions such as drought or cold. However, it can still create glucose for energy through photosynthesis with its bluish-green bark on branches and twigs.

HOW TO SPOT

Height: 20 to 50 feet (6 to 15 m)

Leaves: Main leaf is divided into leaflets; each of these is further divided with 2 to 6 smaller bluish-green leaflets

Seeds: Bright green pods 3 inches (8 cm) long; seeds are flat and tan

North American Range: From southeastern California to central and southwestern Arizona and through the Sonoran Desert

Habitat: Desert regions with streams or creeks and near dry streambeds that can fill with rainwater

HONEY LOCUST
(GLEDITSIA TRIACANTHOS)

The honey locust tree grows well in many environments, including dry areas. Its lower branches usually have reddish thorns with very sharp points. These thorns grow to about eight inches (20 cm) long. Honey locust flowers usually bloom in late spring. The blossoms are greenish yellow. They have a sweet smell that attracts bees. In autumn the tree's leaves turn bright yellow.

HOW TO SPOT

Height: 70 to 80 feet (21 to 24 m)

Leaves: 4 to 8 inches (10 to 20 cm) long; compound leaves made up of dark green oval leaflets

Seeds: Flat, twisted pods 6 to 16 inches (15 to 41 cm) long; seeds inside are surrounded by a sweet pulp

North American Range: Central and eastern United States

Habitat: Moist, fertile soil near streams or lakes

ANIMAL HELPERS

Honey locust seeds are covered with a special coating. The seeds must pass through the gut of an animal to dissolve the coating. Once the animal passes the seeds, the seeds can start to grow into new trees.

KENTUCKY COFFEETREE

(GYMNOCLADUS DIOICUS)

The Kentucky coffeetree has branches that grow in a zigzag pattern. Its greenish-white flowers are about a half inch (1.3 cm) in size. They grow in clusters at the tips of older branches. The flowers appear in late spring to early summer. Also in late spring, new pink leaves begin to grow. They turn bluish green in summer and then yellow in fall. The leaves drop by early fall. The tree does not have leaves most of the year.

HOW TO SPOT

Height: 60 to 90 feet (18 to 27 m)

Leaves: Bluish-green leaves 1 to 3 feet (0.3 to 0.9 m) long and 18 to 24 inches (46 to 61 cm) wide; compound leaves made up of 6 to 14 leaflets

Seeds: Leathery, reddish-brown seed pods containing a few large seeds

North American Range: Midwestern, northeastern, and central United States

Habitat: Floodplains, ravines, and lower slopes

Fruits

FUN FACT

Kentucky coffeetree seeds were used by early European settlers as a substitute for coffee beans.

MEXICAN PALO VERDE

(PARKINSONIA ACULEATA)

The Mexican palo verde is a small tree native to the southern United States and Mexico. It has long branches that are covered in small, thin, green leaflets. The Mexican palo verde is known for its bright yellow flowers. One petal on each flower has reddish-orange marks against the yellow, eventually turning completely reddish orange. Bean-like seed pods develop from these flowers. The tree's leaves drop during summer when the weather is dry. The smooth green bark on its branches can still perform photosynthesis.

HOW TO SPOT

Height: 12 to 33 feet (4 to 10 m)

Leaves: Bright green leaves 15 to 18 inches (38 to 46 cm) long; made up of 10 to 25 pairs of leaflets

Seeds: Seed pods about 3 to 5 inches (8 to 13 cm) long

North American Range: Southern United States and Mexico

Habitat: Hot, sunny locations with well-drained soils in floodplains, bottomlands, and hillsides

BIGLEAF MAGNOLIA

(MAGNOLIA MACROPHYLLA)

The bigleaf magnolia has the largest flowers of any tree in North America. Its flowers bloom from May to July and are highly fragrant. They measure 8 to 14 inches (20 to 36 cm) across. They are creamy white with a slight rose color at the base of the petals. The blooms are often located high off the ground. The leaves do not change color in fall.

HOW TO SPOT

Height: 30 to 40 feet (9 to 12 m)

Leaves: Up to 3 feet (1 m) long and 1 foot (0.3 m) wide; bright green on top and silvery gray and fuzzy underneath

Seeds: Egg-shaped red fruits; 2.5 to 3 inches (6 to 8 cm) long; contain red seeds that hang on thin threads

North American Range: Southeastern United States

Habitat: Wooded areas in river valleys and ravines

MIMOSA *(ALBIZIA JULIBRISSIN)*

The mimosa tree is native to the Middle East and Asia. It was introduced to the United States in 1745 as an ornamental tree. This small tree has a short trunk. The branches spread to form a wide, flat-topped canopy. Pink flowers bloom from May through July. They are made of clusters of silky pink threads and look like small pom-poms. The flowers have a strong, sweet smell. They attract butterflies, bees, and hummingbirds. On cool nights the leaves fold up.

HOW TO SPOT

Height: 20 to 40 feet (6 to 12 m)

Leaves: 6 to 20 inches (15 to 51 cm) long; fern-like with small leaflets

Seeds: Seed pods are about 6 inches (15 cm) long; filled with 5 to 10 hard seeds

North American Range: Central and eastern United States

Habitat: Along roadsides and streams and in forests and clearings

INVASIVE TREES

The mimosa tree is invasive in North America. An invasive species is a non-native species that harms an ecosystem, often by replacing native species. Many native plants are food sources for insects. Invasive species limit these resources by taking nutrients and space native plants need to grow. Invasive species also affect birds, which eat the bugs that feed on native plants.

TULIP TREE *(LIRIODENDRON TULIPIFERA)*

The tulip tree is one of the largest trees in North America. Its name comes from its flowers, which resemble tulips. The flowers bloom in late May or June after the leaves have fully developed. Each flower is about two inches (5 cm) long and has yellowish-green petals. Every petal has an orange band at the base. If broken, the tree's twigs give off a sweet and spicy scent. The leaves turn bright yellowish orange in fall.

HOW TO SPOT

Height: 90 to 200 feet (27 to 61 m)

Leaves: Square-shaped leaves with 3 to 4 lobes; dark green on top and lighter underneath

Seeds: Scaly, cone-shaped brown fruits containing many winged seeds

North American Range: Central and eastern United States

Habitat: Forests with moist soils including bottomlands, mountain coves, and swamps

UMBRELLA MAGNOLIA

(MAGNOLIA TRIPETALA)

The umbrella magnolia got its name from its unusual leaf formation. The leaves grow at the ends of the branches in a circular pattern resembling an umbrella. Large bowl-shaped white flowers bloom in late spring after the leaves appear. Each flower has 6 to 12 narrow petals. Birds enjoy the tree's red fruits. The tree's leaves turn gold in autumn and drop after the first light frost.

HOW TO SPOT

Height: 15 to 40 feet (5 to 12 m)

Leaves: 2 feet (0.6 m) long and 8 inches (20 cm) across; dark green on top and pale green and hairy underneath

Seeds: Cone-like fruits 4 to 6 inches (10 to 15 cm) long with pink or red seeds

North American Range: Throughout the Appalachian Mountains and southeastern United States, as far west as Oklahoma

Habitat: Along mountain streams and creeks and next to swamps

NORTHERN CATALPA

(CATALPA SPECIOSA)

The northern catalpa produces white flowers in May and June. Inside each flower are yellow stripes and small purple spots. The flowers bloom in clusters. Their sweet fragrance attracts bees and hummingbirds. The northern catalpa tree is sometimes called the green bean tree. The shape and color of its seed pods in summer remind some people of green beans.

HOW TO SPOT

Height: 40 to 60 feet (12 to 18 m)

Leaves: Up to 12 inches (30 cm) long; light green, heart-shaped leaves with a fuzzy underside

Seeds: Thin green seed pods that turn brown in fall; pods contain 100 or more winged seeds

North American Range: Ontario, Canada, and central and eastern United States

Habitat: Moist lowlands in forests, along roadsides, and along rivers and lakes

Seed pods

SOUTHERN CATALPA

(CATALPA BIGNONIOIDES)

The southern catalpa has a short, thick trunk and twisting branches. Its bark is thin and breaks into long scales or flakes. White flowers bloom in May and June. They grow in clusters of 10 to 20 flowers. The fruits develop as long pods that look similar to string beans dangling from the branches. The leaves give off an unpleasant smell if crushed. The southern catalpa is the only plant where the catalpa sphinx moth lives. The moth's caterpillars may eat all the leaves on a tree. But new leaves will grow within a month.

HOW TO SPOT

Height: 20 to 40 feet (6 to 12 m)

Leaves: Heart-shaped leaves up to 12 inches (30 cm) long and 4 to 8 inches (10 to 20 cm) wide; smooth on top and paler with fine hairs underneath

Seeds: Dark brown seed pods; each contains many long seeds with a tuft of hair at both ends of each seed

North American Range: Southeastern United States

Habitat: Rich, moist soil along streams and rivers and in floodplains and lowlands

AMERICAN MOUNTAIN ASH

(SORBUS AMERICANA)

The American mountain ash grows well in high, cool places. Despite its name it is not a true ash tree. The leaves of ash trees grow side by side on branches. American mountain ash leaves alternate instead of growing directly across from one another. Between May and July, small white flowers bloom in clusters. The flowers develop into bright red berries. They remain on the tree into winter. The leaves turn yellow and golden orange in fall.

Berries

HOW TO SPOT

Height: 15 to 35 feet (5 to 11 m)

Leaves: 6 to 10 inches (15 to 25 cm) long; compound leaves made up of 9 to 17 dark yellowish-green leaflets with toothed edges

Seeds: Small, bright red berries; each contains 4 seeds

North American Range: Eastern North America from Canada to Georgia

Habitat: Cool, moist, open areas and forests, mountaintops, and ridges

AMUR CHOKECHERRY

(PRUNUS MAACKII)

The Amur chokecherry is native to China, Siberia, and Korea. It is named after the Amur River, which flows between China and Russia. The Amur chokecherry tree usually has more than one trunk. Fragrant white flowers bloom in late spring. They hang in small clusters. The flowers are followed by red fruits that turn black by late summer. The leaves turn yellow in fall and often drop early. In winter, the tree's bark may look shiny and bronze, almost like metal.

HOW TO SPOT

Height: 35 to 45 feet (11 to 14 m)

Leaves: Green oval leaves 2 to 4 inches (5 to 10 cm) long with toothed edges

Seeds: Small black fruits about 0.25 inches (0.6 cm) across; each contains seeds

North American Range: Northern, central, and parts of the northeastern United States

Habitat: Areas with moist, well-drained soil

APPLE *(MALUS PUMILA)*

Apple trees are native to Central Asia and Afghanistan. The many apple varieties have differences in color, flavor, and use. White blossoms tinged with pink bloom in late spring. Some apple varieties ripen in late summer, while others ripen in fall. Ripe apples may be green, yellow, red, or a mixture of these colors.

HOW TO SPOT

Height: 15 to 30 feet (5 to 9 m)

Leaves: Vary in shape and size; raised veins underneath

Seeds: Large, round, firm fruits with a waxy coating; contain 5 seed pockets

North American Range: Throughout the United States, especially in the Pacific Northwest, the Great Lakes region, and the Northeast

Habitat: Thickets, forest edges and openings, fields, pastures, and roadsides

APRICOT *(PRUNUS ARMENIACA)*

The apricot tree is native to eastern Europe and western Asia. Flowers bloom in February and early March. The buds are pink. They turn white after they bloom. Leaves appear after the flowers. Apricot trees begin producing the most fruit when they are three to five years old. The fruits ripen in late June to July. Apricot pits contain poisonous chemicals that can be harmful if the seeds are crushed or chewed.

HOW TO SPOT

Height: 15 to 40 feet (5 to 12 m)

Leaves: Green, egg-shaped leaves with pointed tips and toothed edges; 2 to 3.5 inches (5 to 9 cm) long

Seeds: Yellow to red edible fruits; each has 1 large pit inside

North American Range: Southwestern United States

Habitat: Well-drained soils

Ripe fruits

BLACK CHERRY *(PRUNUS SEROTINA)*

The black cherry tree is the largest native cherry tree in North America. Its bark is gray to black. It has scaly plates with edges that flip upward. If scratched, the twigs give off a bitter almond smell. Small white flowers bloom in April and May. The fruits ripen in clusters of 15 to 30 cherries. They are ripe in August or September. The cherries remain bitter when ripe. In fall, the leaves turn yellow or orange.

HOW TO SPOT

Height: 60 to 80 feet (18 to 24 m)

Leaves: Wide, dark green leaves 3 to 6 inches (8 to 15 cm) long with toothed edges

Seeds: Purplish-black edible fruits, 0.25 to 0.3 inches (0.6 to 0.8 cm) across; each contains 1 seed

North American Range: Midwestern and eastern United States

Habitat: Dry upland sites and along fences, streams, and woodland edges

Ripe fruits

BRADFORD PEAR

(PYRUS CALLERYANA)

The Bradford pear tree is native to eastern Asia, including China, Japan, and Korea. It is often considered an invasive species in the United States. It is one of the first trees to bloom in spring. Creamy white flowers cover the tree, but they have an unpleasant, fishy smell. Bradford pear trees grow quickly and can tolerate city environments well. The leaves may turn gold, orange, red, pink, or purple in fall.

HOW TO SPOT

Height: 30 to 50 feet (9 to 15 m)

Leaves: 3 inches (8 cm) long; dark green on top and pale underneath with rounded teeth

Seeds: Fruits are yellowish green to brown; 0.5 inches (1.3 cm) across with 2 to 4 black seeds

North American Range: From Illinois to Virginia and south to Louisiana and Florida

Habitat: Neighborhoods, roadsides, and forests

FUN FACT

The strong smell from Bradford pear tree flowers attracts flies, including blowflies that pollinate the tree.

Fruits

ROSE FAMILY

COMMON PEAR *(PYRUS COMMUNIS)*

The common pear tree is native to Europe and northern Iraq. The many varieties of this tree produce fruits of different shapes, sizes, and colors. The branches of pear trees are sometimes spiny. White flowers bloom in clusters in spring. Edible fruits grow from the flowers. The fruits ripen between midsummer and fall. The leaves turn shades of red or yellow in fall.

Ripe fruits

HOW TO SPOT

Height: 40 to 60 feet (12 to 18 m)

Leaves: Oval green leaves; 1 to 4 inches (2.5 to 10 cm) long with toothed edges

Seeds: Most fruits are shaped like a teardrop; fruits contain small brown seeds

North American Range: Grows naturally in the eastern United States and grown for food through North America

Habitat: Fields, roadsides, forest borders, and open woodland areas

EUROPEAN MOUNTAIN ASH

(SORBUS AUCUPARIA)

The European mountain ash is native to Europe, North Africa, and western Asia. Young trees have smooth bark that becomes scaly as they grow older. The European mountain ash often has more than one trunk. The branches may start close to the ground. Small white flowers bloom in large clusters in May. The fruits appear in late summer to early fall. Also in fall, the leaves turn yellow to reddish purple.

HOW TO SPOT

Height: 20 to 40 feet (6 to 12 m)

Leaves: Compound leaves 5 to 9 inches (13 to 23 cm) long; 9 to 15 oval leaflets with toothed edges; dark green on top and paler underneath

Seeds: Small, red fruits grow in clusters; each contains several seeds

North American Range: Southern Canada and northern United States

Habitat: Moist forests, fields, and roadsides in cooler climates

Fruits

JAPANESE CHERRY

(PRUNUS SERRULATA)

The Japanese cherry tree is native to Japan, Korea, and China. Different varieties of this tree have been developed for their flowers. The flowers range from white to dark pink. They bloom between March and May. Some Japanese cherry tree varieties produce small cherries in summer, but people usually do not eat these because they are so sour. The trees have smooth, shiny, reddish-brown bark with long raised openings.

HOW TO SPOT

Height: 15 to 25 feet (5 to 8 m)

Leaves: Dark green oval leaves; 2 to 5 inches (5 to 13 cm) long with toothed edges

Seeds: Small, round, pea-sized fruits about 0.4 inches (1 cm) across, each with a single seed

North American Range: California and midwestern and eastern United States

Habitat: Moist and well-drained soil

FUN FACT

In 1912, the Japanese government sent 3,000 cherry trees to the US government as a gift. The trees were planted in Washington, DC.

MEXICAN PLUM *(PRUNUS MEXICANA)*

The Mexican plum is a small, slow-growing tree. It is known for its fragrant white flowers. Small clusters of flowers cover the tree in April and May. The flowers develop into fruits in summer. As the fruits ripen, they turn from yellow to pink to dark purple. They are ready to harvest in September. The fruits are tart, but people use them to make jams and jellies. In fall the tree's leaves turn yellow, orange, or red.

HOW TO SPOT

Height: 10 to 35 feet (3 to 11 m)

Leaves: Yellowish-green leaves; 2 to 4 inches (5 to 10 cm) long with toothed edges; shiny on top and fuzzy underneath

Seeds: Dark purplish-red edible fruits, each with a bluish powdery coating and a single seed inside

North American Range: Central and southeastern United States and northeastern Mexico

Habitat: Moist slopes, creek bottoms, canyons, fencerows, and woodlands

PEACH *(PRUNUS PERSICA)*

Peach trees are native to Asia and have many varieties. They often have more than one trunk. Their fragrant pink flowers bloom alone or in pairs. The flowers are about one to 1.5 inches (2.5 to 4 cm) long. The trees produce fruits in summer. The juicy fruits are edible, but the seeds and leaves are poisonous. In fall the leaves turn yellow. As the trees get older, their gray bark becomes rough and scaly.

Ripe fruits

HOW TO SPOT

Height: 15 to 25 feet (5 to 8 m)

Leaves: 3 to 6 inches (8 to 15 cm) with toothed edges; leaves come to a point

Seeds: Fuzzy yellow to orange fruits tinged with red, each with 1 large, rough seed

North American Range: Ontario, Canada, and eastern and southern United States

Habitat: Forest edges and roadsides

PIN CHERRY *(PRUNUS PENSYLVANICA)*

Pin cherry trees are fast-growing, slender trees. Their branches have shiny red twigs. Clusters of fragrant white flowers bloom from late March to early June. The bark and leaves also give off a scent. The thin, smooth bark is reddish brown with horizontal bands of orange to red dots. The fruits appear in clusters with long stems. They mature in late summer and fall.

HOW TO SPOT

Height: 25 to 40 feet (8 to 12 m)

Leaves: Dark yellowish-green oval leaves 3 to 5 inches (8 to 13 cm) long with toothed edges and a pointed tip; shiny on top and lighter underneath

Seeds: Small, shiny red berries, 0.25 inches (0.6 cm) across with 1 seed in the center

North American Range: Northern and eastern North America and the midwestern United States

Habitat: Open woods, forest edges, fields, and roadsides

FUN FACT

The pin cherry tree is often called the fire cherry. It is one of the first trees to regrow after a fire.

SWEET CHERRY *(PRUNUS AVIUM)*

The sweet cherry tree is native to Europe and northern Africa. It has a single straight trunk. Fragrant white flowers bloom in April before the leaves emerge. The flowers are about one to three inches (2.5 to 8 cm) long. They grow alone or in clusters. Depending on the climate, the fruits ripen between May and July. As they become ripe, the fruits darken to black and sweeten. The leaves of the sweet cherry tree turn yellow in fall.

HOW TO SPOT

Height: 15 to 30 feet (5 to 9 m)

Leaves: Oval leaves 2 to 5 inches (5 to 13 cm) long with toothed edges

Seeds: Yellow, red, or purple fruits that are soft and juicy; fruits are attached to a long stem and have 1 large seed inside

North American Range: Midwestern and eastern North America

Habitat: Forests, ravines, clearings, and floodplains

SWEET CRABAPPLE

(MALUS CORONARIA)

Sweet crabapple trees get their name from the sweet fragrance of their flowers and fruits, not the taste of the fruits. The flowers are white to pink and bloom in April, May, and June. The fruits develop in summer. They are bitter to taste, although they can be used to make jelly. Sweet crabapple trees often have multiple trunks. The branches jut out at different angles and can appear tangled. The branches near the center may die if the outer branches block out sunlight.

FUN FACT

The main difference between a crabapple and an apple is size. Crabapples are a maximum of two inches (5 cm) in diameter. Anything larger is an apple.

HOW TO SPOT

Height: 35 feet (11 m)

Leaves: Triangular or oval with toothed edges; 2.5 to 4 inches (6 to 10 cm) long

Seeds: Small yellow fruits 0.75 to 1.5 inches (2 to 4 cm) across; smooth and waxy outer skin, juicy and sour inside with several seeds in the center

North American Range: Ontario, Canada, and midwestern and eastern United States

Habitat: Open fields, woodland edges, and stream banks

RED MULBERRY *(MORUS RUBRA)*

The red mulberry tree has a short trunk and a thick, widespread canopy. The flowers form in small, slim, hanging clusters. They bloom from March to April. The fruits mature about two months later. The berries are sweet and juicy. People may eat them off the tree. However, the berries spoil quickly, so they are not often sold in stores. In fall the tree's leaves turn bright yellow.

HOW TO SPOT

Height: 25 to 60 feet (8 to 18 m)

Leaves: Dark green, oval leaves 3 to 5 inches (8 to 13 cm) long; may have lobes; rough on top and hairy underneath with toothed edges

Seeds: Dark purple, sweet, blackberry-like edible fruits 1 to 1.5 inches (2.5 to 4 cm) long

North American Range: Southeastern Canada and central and eastern United States

Habitat: Woods, bottomlands, riverbanks, ditches, and ravines

WHITE MULBERRY *(MORUS ALBA)*

The white mulberry tree is native to China. It is sometimes considered an invasive tree in North America. It can take over the habitat of native red mulberry trees. The white mulberry has a short trunk and many small, slender branches and twigs. The branches are reddish brown and turn gray as the tree grows older. Flowers bloom from April to May in small, tight clusters. In fall the leaves turn yellow before they drop.

Berries

HOW TO SPOT

Height: 30 to 60 feet (9 to 18 m)

Leaves: Smooth dark green leaves; 2 to 6 inches (5 to 15 cm) long; may have up to 5 lobes with toothed edges and a pointed tip

Seeds: White, pink, or purple blackberry-like fruits about 1.5 inches (4 cm) long

North American Range: Southern Canada and every US state except Alaska, Hawaii, and Nevada

Habitat: Fields, pastures, and along fences and streams

BITTERNUT HICKORY

(CARYA CORDIFORMIS)

The bitternut hickory tree has a canopy of branches that reach upward. The lower branches droop toward the ground. Small flowers bloom in late spring. Leaves often stay green in fall but will sometimes turn yellow. The fruits mature in fall. The fruits' thin outer coverings split into four parts to release very bitter nuts. From midsummer until the following spring, the tree's branches have buds covered with bright yellow dots and small hairs.

HOW TO SPOT

Height: 50 to 100 feet (15 to 30 m)

Leaves: 6 to 12 inches (15 to 30 cm) long; 7 to 11 leaflets with toothed edges; smooth on top and slightly hairy underneath

Seeds: Yellowish-green husks with scruffy hairs; each contains 1 nut

North American Range: Eastern Canada and central and eastern United States

Habitat: Woods along streams, rivers, and swamps

BLACK WALNUT *(JUGLANS NIGRA)*

Most parts of the black walnut give off a strong smell when rubbed or cut. Flowers bloom in spring. The leaves are green in summer and change to yellow in fall. If there is not much rain, the leaves begin dropping in summer. During wetter years, the leaves drop later in the season. In fall the husks of the tree's fruits become blacker as they ripen. The nuts inside are oily and sweet.

FUN FACT

If people pick up ripe black walnuts, a dark dye from the husk will stain their skin.

HOW TO SPOT

Height: 50 to 100 feet (15 to 30 m) or taller

Leaves: 1 to 2 feet (0.3 to 0.6 m) long; 15 to 23 oval leaflets with toothed edges

Seeds: Yellowish-black husks; each contain an edible nut

North American Range: Midwestern, eastern, and Great Plains regions of the United States

Habitat: Moist, well-drained soil in bottomlands and fields

Young fruits

BUTTERNUT *(JUGLANS CINEREA)*

The butternut tree has a short trunk and branches that grow upward. It cannot survive in the shade. It does not compete well with other trees that may block out sunlight. The butternut's flowers bloom from April to June, depending on location. Husks grow in clusters in summer. In fall the leaves turn yellow and brown. The husks stay on the tree until after the leaves drop. People and animals eat the nuts inside.

HOW TO SPOT

Height: 40 to 60 feet (12 to 18 m)

Leaves: 10 to 20 inches (25 to 51 cm) long; compound leaves with 11 to 19 leaflets; yellowish green with fine hairs on top

Seeds: Sticky husks with brown hairs and a strong odor contain light brown, sweet, oily nuts

North American Range: Southeastern Canada into northeastern United States, ending just west of the Mississippi

Habitat: Along streams and in moist woods at the bases of slopes and hills; along streams

MOCKERNUT HICKORY

(CARYA TOMENTOSA)

The mockernut hickory is a strong tree with a straight trunk. Leaf stems are covered with hairs that give off a spicy orange smell if cut or bruised. Each tree has both male and female flowers. The flowers bloom from April to May. Mockernut hickories do not produce nuts until they are about 25 years old. After that they can continue to produce for more than 200 years. The nuts are very hard to crack. The tree's leaves turn yellow in fall.

HOW TO SPOT

Height: 50 to 150 feet (15 to 46 m)

Leaves: 8 to 15 inches (20 to 38 cm) long; compound leaves of 5 to 9 leaflets with toothed edges; shiny yellowish green on top and paler with dense hairs underneath

Seeds: Husks have 4 segments that turn brown when mature; each husk contains a single hickory nut

North American Range: Central and eastern United States

Habitat: Dry upland woods on upper slopes and ridges

Husks

NUTMEG HICKORY

(CARYA MYRISTICIFORMIS)

The nutmeg hickory is the rarest of hickory trees. It grows slowly. Some nutmeg hickories take 20 years to grow the first 30 feet (9 m). The tree's leaves emerge in early spring. Tiny silver scales cover the underside of each leaf. The leaves stay shiny throughout spring until they turn yellow in fall. The tree's nuts are ripe by late fall. They are small and taste sweet.

Nuts

HOW TO SPOT

Height: 80 to 100 feet (24 to 30 m)

Leaves: 7 to 14 inches (18 to 36 cm) long with 5 to 9 leaflets; green on top and shiny silver underneath; toothed edges

Seeds: Nuts about 1 inch (2.5 cm) long with a thick shell

North American Range: From the coasts of North and South Carolina to the mountains of northeastern Mexico

Habitat: Riverbanks, swamps, bottomlands, and sometimes hillsides

PECAN *(CARYA ILLINOINENSIS)*

The pecan tree is one of the last trees to grow twigs or leaves in spring. The branches of a pecan tree spread up and out from the trunk. Lower branches may sweep downward. The yellowish-green flowers bloom in spring. In fall the pecan husks split into four sections, revealing the nut. Also in fall the pecan tree's leaves turn golden yellow.

HOW TO SPOT

Height: 70 to 130 feet (21 to 40 m)

Leaves: 4 to 8 inches (10 to 20 cm) long; compound leaves with 9 to 17 leaflets with toothed edges; dark green above and paler underneath

Seeds: Husks contain a sweet tan or brown oval nut 1 to 3 inches (2.5 to 8 cm) long with dark streaks

North American Range: Midwestern and southern United States and parts of California

Habitat: Moist, well-drained soils along rivers and in bottomland woods

Husks and nut

FUN FACT

Albany, Georgia, is called the pecan capital of the United States. The city has more than 600,000 pecan trees.

PIGNUT HICKORY *(CARYA GLABRA)*

The pignut hickory is a strong tree with a straight trunk. Yellow male and female flowers grow on the same tree. The male flowers bloom in hanging catkins. The female flowers bloom on short spikes and develop into hickory nuts. Pignut hickory trees are usually 25 to 30 years old before they begin producing nuts. The tree has thin gray bark with crisscrossing cracks that form diamond shapes. The leaves of the pignut hickory turn yellow in fall.

FUN FACT

Pignut hickory nuts taste bitter. Early European settlers fed them to pigs, giving the tree its name.

HOW TO SPOT

Height: 50 to 120 feet (15 to 37 m)

Leaves: 8 to 12 inches (20 to 30 cm) long; 5 to 7 leaflets with toothed edges; yellowish green on top and lighter underneath

Seeds: Dark brown oval husks with a tan-colored nut inside

North American Range: Southeastern Canada and central and eastern United States

Habitat: Dry upland woods and ridges

SHAGBARK HICKORY *(CARYA OVATA)*

The shagbark hickory has large, flat, curving plates of bark that peel away, giving the tree a shaggy appearance. It has a straight trunk with branches that form an oval canopy. Shagbark hickories begin producing seeds when they are about 40 years old. Flowers bloom in April and May. Husks develop later and ripen in September and October. The husks split open into four sections when they are ripe. The leaves turn yellow to brown before they drop in fall.

HOW TO SPOT

Height: 60 to 120 feet (18 to 37 m)

Leaves: 8 to 15 inches (20 to 38 cm) long; compound leaves with 5 toothed leaflets

Seeds: Hard outer husks with edible nuts inside

North American Range: Midwestern and eastern United States

Habitat: Moist areas in forests

BEECH FAMILY

AMERICAN BEECH

(FAGUS GRANDIFOLIA)

The American beech tree has a short trunk and wide, low-growing branches. Yellowish-green flowers bloom from March to May. Male flowers form in drooping clusters. Female flowers grow on the same tree in short spikes. Fruits ripen in fall and have prickly husks. Inside are hard, edible beechnuts. The husks stay on the tree after the nuts have fallen. Leaves turn gold in fall. They usually drop late in winter.

HOW TO SPOT

Height: 50 to 70 feet (15 to 21 m)

Leaves: 2 to 5 inches (5 to 13 cm) long; egg shaped with toothed edges; dark green on top and lighter underneath

Seeds: A prickly husk holds a single three-sided, shiny brown nut

North American Range: Eastern North America

Habitat: Cooler areas, such as slopes and ravines

AMERICAN CHESTNUT

(CASTANEA DENTATA)

The American chestnut was once the largest and most plentiful tree in eastern North America. In 1904, trees in New York became infected with chestnut blight. This disease spread and killed billions of American chestnut trees. Today American chestnut trees are hard to find in the wild, and wild trees die before they reach full height. On mature trees, pale white flowers bloom in June and July. They develop into large green husks with spiny coverings. Inside are nuts people and animals eat. The leaves turn yellow in fall.

HOW TO SPOT

Height: 50 to 100 feet (15 to 30 m) or taller

Leaves: Long and canoe shaped with toothed edges

Seeds: Spiny capsules with 3 nuts inside each husk

North American Range: Eastern North America, especially the Appalachian Mountains

Habitat: Forests and mountain slopes

BRINGING BACK THE AMERICAN CHESTNUT

Scientists are working on ways to help American chestnut trees grow in the wild. They are trying to make the trees more resistant to chestnut blight. One method is to cross American chestnut trees with Chinese chestnut trees. Another is to add a gene from wheat to the trees. So far these attempts have not been successful.

CHERRYBARK OAK

(QUERCUS PAGODA)

The cherrybark oak has a straight trunk and round, broad canopy. The tree gets its species name, *pagoda*, from the appearance of its leaves. When the tip of a leaf is pointed toward the ground, the leaf resembles a pagoda. The tree's flowers grow at the same time as the leaves in spring. Male and female flowers bloom on the same tree. The tree has acorns that take two years to mature. In fall the leaves turn yellowish brown before they drop.

HOW TO SPOT

Height: 90 to 130 feet (27 to 40 m)

Leaves: Dark green leaves 5 to 8 inches (13 to 20 cm) long with 5 to 11 pointed lobes; smooth and shiny on top and paler with hairs underneath

Seeds: Acorns are 0.5 inches (1.3 cm) long with a brownish-orange, scaly cap that covers one-third of the nut

North American Range: Along the Atlantic Coast from Virginia to Florida and from the Gulf Coast to eastern Texas

Habitat: Well-drained soil along streams and in bottomlands

NORTHERN RED OAK

(QUERCUS RUBRA)

The northern red oak has a canopy with branches that start close to the ground. Male and female flowers bloom in spring. Acorns appear in fall. The tree begins producing acorns when it is about 25 years old. However, it does not produce many acorns until it is about 50 years old. The acorns remain on the tree for two years. They drop in late summer or early fall, when the leaves turn a reddish brown.

HOW TO SPOT

Height: 50 to 90 feet (15 to 27 m)

Leaves: 5 to 8 inches (13 to 20 cm) long with 7 to 11 lobes with bristle tips; green on top and grayish white underneath

Seeds: Acorns are 0.75 to 1.5 inches (2 to 4 cm) long; the flat, wide cap covers one-fourth of the acorn

North American Range: From Nova Scotia to Ontario in Canada and from Minnesota to North Carolina and Georgia in the United States

Habitat: Coves, ravines, valleys, and mid- to low slopes

Acorns

OVERCUP OAK *(QUERCUS LYRATA)*

The overcup oak is a slow-growing tree. It can live for 400 years. Its canopy is formed of small, twisted branches. Flowers bloom in spring. The acorns that follow ripen by September or October. They have a unique spongy shell that allows them to float in water. Streams can carry these acorns long distances. The tree's leaves turn yellow to brown in fall. The leaves drop from the tree much earlier than the leaves of other oaks.

HOW TO SPOT

Height: 60 to 90 feet (18 to 27 m)

Leaves: 6 to 8 inches (15 to 20 cm) long; shiny dark green on top and lighter grayish green with hairs underneath; wedge shaped with 5 to 9 lobes

Seeds: Light brown acorns up to 1 inch (2.5 cm) long; the nut is almost entirely covered by the cap

North American Range: East coast of the United States from New Jersey to Florida and west to Texas

Habitat: Wet areas including bottomland forests, swamps, and floodplains, and along streams and rivers

FUN FACT

Many types of water birds eat overcup oak acorns as they float downstream.

Acorns

OZARK CHINQUAPIN

(CASTANEA OZARKENSIS)

The Ozark chinquapin tree does not often grow more than 30 feet (9 m) tall. This is because chestnut blight kills many Ozark chinquapin trees before they can grow to their full height. Young trees have smooth, dark gray bark with silver markings. Later the bark develops flat, wide, plate-like ridges. On mature trees, flowers appear in catkins in late May to June. The flowers are creamy white and smell fishy. In fall spiny burs develop. Each bur is about the size of a golf ball. It contains an edible, sweet nut. The leaves turn yellow in fall.

HOW TO SPOT

Height: 60 to 65 feet (18 to 20 m)

Leaves: Yellowish-green leaves; 5.5 to 9.5 inches (14 to 24 cm) long with toothed edges

Seeds: Spiny burs 1.25 inches (3 cm) long; each contains 1 small, round seed

North American Range: Ozark and Ouachita Mountains in the central and southeastern United States

Habitat: Rocky slopes, ridges, and woods

Catkins

PIN OAK *(QUERCUS PALUSTRIS)*

The pin oak has branches that grow in a unique pattern. Lower branches droop downward. Middle branches grow straight out to the side. Branches at the top slant upward. Male flowers grow in drooping yellow clusters. Female flowers grow on short spikes. The acorns take 16 to 18 months to develop. They grow alone or in clusters of two to three. Leaves turn orange or red in fall. Young trees keep their leaves through winter. The new, lower branches of older trees keep their leaves too.

HOW TO SPOT

Height: 50 to 100 feet (15 to 30 m)

Leaves: Glossy, dark green leaves; 4 to 6 inches (10 to 15 cm) long; 5 to 9 lobes with 2 to 5 teeth

Seeds: Round, reddish-brown acorns about 0.25 to 0.5 inches (0.6 to 1.3 cm) across; often striped; smooth, thin cap covers about one-fourth of the nut

North American Range: Southeastern Canada and north-central and northeastern United States

Habitat: Marshes, swamps, and wet bottomlands

SCARLET OAK *(QUERCUS COCCINEA)*

The scarlet oak is best known for its bright red fall leaves. Its branches reach upward and do not droop. The trunk often flares out at the base. If the tree is growing too close to a sidewalk, its trunk and roots may lift the concrete. The scarlet oak grows quickly compared to other oak trees. Its acorns are an important food source for many animals including squirrels, chipmunks, mice, deer, and birds.

HOW TO SPOT

Height: 50 to 80 feet (15 to 24 m)

Leaves: 3 to 7 inches (8 to 18 cm) long; shiny green above and lighter underneath; C-shaped, pointed lobes

Seeds: Acorns about 0.5 to 1 inch (1.3 to 2.5 cm) long with a bowl-shaped cap that covers one-half of each nut

North American Range: North-central and eastern United States

Habitat: Dry and sandy soils, especially along ridges and slopes

SHINGLE OAK *(QUERCUS IMBRICARIA)*

The shingle oak has widely spread lower branches and upright upper branches. Flowers grow in spring just before the leaves fully emerge. Unlike many other oak trees, the leaves do not have lobes. When the leaves first grow, they have a red to yellow color. During summer the leaves turn a deep, rich green. In fall they turn yellow or reddish brown. Acorns ripen in early to midfall. They take two years to mature.

HOW TO SPOT

Height: 50 to 70 feet (15 to 21 m); may grow up to 100 feet (30 m)

Leaves: Oval leaves; 3 to 6 inches (8 to 15 cm) long with no lobes and 1 bristle; glossy green on top and paler underneath

Seeds: Round acorns about 0.5 to 0.75 inches (1.3 to 2 cm) long with thin, scaly caps covering about one-third of the nut

North American Range: Midwestern and eastern United States

Habitat: Near streams or riverbanks

SOUTHERN LIVE OAK

(QUERCUS VIRGINIANA)

The southern live oak has a large, short trunk that divides into huge twisting branches. The branches form a low, large canopy. White Spanish moss often hangs from the branches. Yellow flowers grow in drooping clusters in spring. Acorns appear in fall and take one year to mature. The leaves remain on the tree throughout winter. They drop just as new leaves emerge in spring. This makes the southern live oak appear to be evergreen.

HOW TO SPOT

Height: 40 to 80 feet (12 to 24 m)

Leaves: Wide oval leaves; 2 to 4 inches (5 to 10 cm) long; glossy and dark green on top and a paler silvery white underneath

Seeds: Shiny, dark brown, egg-shaped acorns about 1 inch (2.5 cm) long with a gray, fuzzy cap

North American Range: Southeastern United States to Texas and Oklahoma

Habitat: Sandy coastal plains

LIVE OAKS FOR THE US NAVY

Live oak wood is very hard and strong. It is also resistant to decay. That makes the wood a good building material for wooden sailing ships. In 1826 President John Quincy Adams set aside a group of live oaks in Florida for the US Navy to use. Some of these trees are still growing in the Naval Live Oak area of the Gulf Islands National Seashore.

SWAMP WHITE OAK

(QUERCUS BICOLOR)

The swamp white oak has a two-layer root system. This allows the tree to grow in areas that may be flooded in spring but dry in summer. Surface roots collect water when the land is flooded. Deeper roots can reach water farther down when there is little rain. Swamp white oaks begin producing seeds when they are about 20 years old. Leaves turn orange to yellow in fall.

HOW TO SPOT

Height: 50 to 60 feet (15 to 18 m)

Leaves: 5 to 7 inches (13 to 18 cm) long with shallow lobes; dark green on top and silvery white underneath

Seeds: Acorns are about 1 inch (2.5 cm) long and covered halfway with a cap

North American Range: Northeastern North America

Habitat: Low-lying areas, swamps, moist bottomlands, and riverbanks

TURKEY OAK *(QUERCUS LAEVIS)*

The turkey oak is named for its leaves. Many of the leaves have three lobes at the end that look similar to a turkey's foot. The leaves hang down toward the ground. Flowers bloom in April. The male flowers grow in hanging clusters. The clusters are three to five inches (8 to 13 cm) long. Female flowers grow either alone or in pairs. The tree produces acorns every year in September and October. However, the acorns take two years to mature. The tree's leaves turn bright red to brown in fall. They often stay on the tree into winter.

HOW TO SPOT

Height: 30 to 40 feet (9 to 12 m)

Leaves: 4 to 8 inches (10 to 20 cm) long with 3 to 7 lobes; shiny green on top with bristled tips

Seeds: Brown acorns 1 inch (2.5 cm) long with thin reddish-brown caps with fuzzy scales; caps cover one-third of each nut

North American Range: Southeastern United States

Habitat: Dry, sandy, and well-drained soils on ridges

WHITE OAK *(QUERCUS ALBA)*

The white oak tree is a huge, slow-growing tree. It has a long, straight trunk with widespread branches. It grows approximately one foot (0.3 m) each year. Its bark is gray to tan with shallow furrows; thick, flat, plates; and flat ridges. Large sections of bark on the trunk may be smooth due to a harmless fungus growing on the tree. Acorns mature every year. The leaves of the white oak turn a purplish-brown color in fall. They drop halfway through winter.

HOW TO SPOT

Height: 50 to 135 feet (15 to 41 m)

Leaves: 4 to 9 inches (10 to 23 cm) long; each leaf has 5 to 9 lobes with rounded tips; bright green on top and white underneath

Seeds: Light brown acorns are 1 inch (2.5 cm) long with a lumpy cap

North American Range: Eastern United States

Habitat: Dry slopes, valleys, and ravines

WILLOW OAK *(QUERCUS PHELLOS)*

The willow oak is a fast-growing tree. It has a round canopy made up of many thin branches. The branches droop as the tree grows. The leaves of the willow oak look similar to those of willow trees. They are narrow and do not have lobes. The tips of willow oak leaves have bristles. Flowers bloom on the willow oak for one to two weeks in midspring. The acorns take two years to develop. In fall the leaves turn a pale yellow color.

HOW TO SPOT

Height: 60 to 100 feet (18 to 30 m)

Leaves: Oval leaves 2 to 5 inches (5 to 13 cm) long with smooth edges; shiny light green on top and paler underneath with tiny bristle tips

Seeds: Round acorns are about 0.5 inches (1.3 cm) long with shallow caps

North American Range: Southeastern United States

Habitat: Woods near swamps, streams, or lakes

AMERICAN ELM *(ULMUS AMERICANA)*

The American elm tree can grow in three different forms. The branches may droop at the ends, creating a canopy shaped like a vase. The branches may spread wide without drooping. Or short branches may cover the trunk. In spring, small greenish-red flowers appear before the leaves develop. The flowers give way to clusters of seeds on long stems. The tree grows samaras. These small, dry fruits have flat, wing-like structures that allow them to be carried by the wind. In fall the tree's leaves change to yellow.

HOW TO SPOT

Height: 60 to 80 feet (18 to 24 m)

Leaves: Dark green, pointed oval leaves that are shorter on 1 side; 4 to 6 inches (10 to 15 cm) long with toothed edges

Seeds: Flat, oval samaras that each contain 1 tiny seed

North American Range: Central United States and eastern North America

Habitat: Stream banks and lowland areas

ROCK ELM *(ULMUS THOMASII)*

The rock elm tree has one main trunk that grows straight and tall. The branches form high on the tree, creating a narrow canopy. Older branches often have thick, cork-like ridges. Greenish-red flowers bloom anytime from March to May. They grow in small clusters. Two weeks after the flowers bloom, the leaves appear. Samaras develop in May. The tree's leaves turn gold in fall.

HOW TO SPOT

Height: 80 to 100 feet (24 to 30 m)

Leaves: 2 to 4 inches (5 to 10 cm) long with toothed edges; dark green, shiny, and smooth on top and light green and hairy underneath

Seeds: Hairy samaras 0.5 inches (1.3 cm) long with 1 wing; each contains 1 seed

North American Range: Southern Canada and midwestern, northeastern, and southeastern United States

Habitat: Bottomlands and at the base of moist, wooded slopes

SLIPPERY ELM *(ULMUS RUBRA)*

The slippery elm is named for its slick, sticky inner bark. It is one of the first trees to bloom in spring. Its flowers appear before the leaves. The flowers are greenish red and difficult to notice. The tree's samaras ripen from April to June. The leaves have hairs on both sides. This gives them a rough texture that is similar to sandpaper. In fall the leaves turn yellow.

HOW TO SPOT

Height: 40 to 70 feet (12 to 21 m)

Leaves: 4 to 8 inches (10 to 20 cm) long with a toothed edge; dark green on top and lighter underneath

Seeds: Flat samaras with 1 seed each

North American Range: Central and eastern United States

Habitat: Lower slopes, streambanks, bottomlands, and floodplains

Samaras

FUN FACT

Some American Indian peoples used the sweet inner bark of slippery elm trees as medicine. For example, Ojibwe people used it to treat sore throats.

WINGED ELM *(ULMUS ALATA)*

The winged elm is a fast-growing tree. Its branches rise and then bend toward the ground. The tree has corky, wing-like pieces along opposite sides of the branches. The wings are different sizes from one tree to another. The winged elm has small brownish-green flowers that grow in clusters. They bloom from late winter to early spring. The leaves turn yellow in fall.

HOW TO SPOT

Height: 40 to 90 feet (12 to 27 m)

Leaves: 2 to 4 inches (5 to 10 cm) long with toothed edges; dark green on top and paler underneath

Seeds: Samaras about 0.3 inches (0.8 cm) long covered with light-colored fuzz and 2 curving bristles on the end

North American Range: Central and eastern North America

Habitat: Dry, rocky ridges and moist soils along streams and swamps

HACKBERRY *(CELTIS OCCIDENTALIS)*

The hackberry tree has a straight trunk and spreading branches. The branches usually droop at the tips. Flowers bloom in April and May with yellowish-green petals. The male flowers grow in clusters, and the female flowers grow alone. The female flowers develop into the tree's berry-like fruits. The fruits ripen in late summer. They turn dark purple later in fall. Also in fall the leaves turn yellow.

HOW TO SPOT

Height: 40 to 130 feet (12 to 40 m)

Leaves: Green, pointed oval leaves; 2 to 4 inches (5 to 10 cm) long with small teeth along the edges

Seeds: Dark purple berry-like fruits, each containing 1 round brown seed

North American Range: Midwestern to northeastern United States

Habitat: Along rivers and streams, in open woodlands, and on rocky hillsides

Fruits

SUGARBERRY *(CELTIS LAEVIGATA)*

The sugarberry is a fast-growing tree. Young trees have smooth, light gray bark. As trees grow older the bark develops bumps known as warts. The sugarberry has spreading branches that form a wide canopy. This tree can grow in poor conditions, such as in places with little water and high temperatures. Its flowers appear in April and May. Fruits appear from August to October. Parts of the fruits are edible and sweet. The leaves turn bright yellow in fall.

HOW TO SPOT

Height: 50 to 70 feet (15 to 21 m)

Leaves: 2 to 4 inches (5 to 10 cm) long and slender; light green on top and paler underneath

Seeds: Red or purple fruits, each containing 1 round brown seed

North American Range: Southeastern United States

Habitat: Woodlands, floodplains, bottomlands, and wet ground along streams

Leaves and fruits

AMERICAN SYCAMORE

(PLATANUS OCCIDENTALIS)

The American sycamore is a large, fast-growing tree. It has a huge trunk with crooked, widespread branches. The leaves are usually wider than they are long. Small flowers appear in clusters in spring. Male flowers are greenish yellow, and female flowers are red. The flowers develop into round fruits. These ripen and turn brown in fall. When the fruits fall to the ground, they split open to release seeds. The leaves turn yellow to brown in fall.

FUN FACT

Many of the largest American sycamores are hollow. Some European settlers used these trees to shelter their animals.

HOW TO SPOT

Height: 75 to 100 feet (23 to 30 m)

Leaves: Large, egg-shaped leaves with 3 to 5 lobes and toothed edges; 4 to 9 inches (10 to 23 cm) wide

Seeds: Fuzzy, round, brown balls about 1 inch (2.5 cm) across containing seed-like structures

North American Range: Southeastern Canada, central and eastern United States, and northeastern Mexico

Habitat: Moist woods, floodplains, and bottomlands, and along waterways

CALIFORNIA SYCAMORE

(PLATANUS RACEMOSA)

The California sycamore has a short, strong trunk. The trunk often divides into thick, twisting branches. Leaves and flowers first appear in late winter. The tiny red flowers form into round balls. Three to seven balls hang on a stalk. They develop into clusters of tufted seeds. When the seeds are mature, the clusters break off. The wind catches the tufts on the seeds, carrying them long distances.

HOW TO SPOT

Height: 50 to 80 feet (15 to 24 m)

Leaves: Fuzzy star-shaped leaves; 5 to 10 inches (13 to 25 cm) long with 3 to 5 lobes

Seeds: Seed balls the size of golf balls containing seeds with short, brown hairs

North American Range: South-central California and Baja California, Mexico

Habitat: Wetlands, along streams, in floodplains, and along canyons

Seed balls

BLACK ASH *(FRAXINUS NIGRA)*

The black ash tree has a narrow, tall trunk. Its branches start high up on the trunk, sometimes up to 50 feet (15 m) high. Yellow flowers bloom in spring. The flowers grow in tight clusters that are one to two inches (2.5 to 5 cm) long. The fruits also grow in clusters. They often have a spicy smell. Leaves turn yellow and drop in early fall. The seed clusters may stay on the tree throughout winter.

HOW TO SPOT

Height: 40 to 90 feet (12 to 27 m)

Leaves: 10 to 16 inches (25 to 41 cm) long; 7 to 13 leaflets with toothed edges; dark green on top and paler underneath

Seeds: Samaras 1 to 1.5 inches (2.5 to 4 cm) long with paddle-shaped wings; each contains 1 to 3 flat seeds

North American Range: Eastern Canada and northeastern United States

Habitat: Forests, swamps, and floodplains

BLUE ASH *(FRAXINUS QUADRANGULATA)*

The blue ash tree has gray bark with shaggy or scaly plates. Its twigs are square instead of round. They may be winged. Flowers bloom in spring. Blue ash trees have both male and female flowers, so every tree can bear fruits. The tree's samaras grow in clusters. New seeds develop every three to four years. The blue ash does not have showy fall colors. Instead, its leaves are often pale yellow or green in fall.

HOW TO SPOT

Height: 50 to 150 feet (15 to 46 m)

Leaves: Leaves have 5 to 11 oval leaflets that are 2 to 5 inches (5 to 13 cm) long

Seeds: Samaras 1 to 3 inches (2.5 to 8 cm) long

North American Range: Midwestern United States

Habitat: Rocky slopes

FUN FACT

The blue ash tree's name is a reference to blue dye produced from its inner bark. The bark releases the dye when crushed and soaked in water.

GREEN ASH *(FRAXINUS PENNSYLVANICA)*

Green ash trees have a round canopy made of slender, spreading branches. Male and female flowers grow on separate trees. The flowers do not have petals. The male flowers are light green to purple and grow in tight clusters. The female flowers are green and grow in drooping clusters. The female flowers develop into samaras. The samaras may hang on through winter. When they drop, wind carries them away. The tree's leaves turn yellow in fall.

Samaras

HOW TO SPOT

Height: 50 to 70 feet (15 to 21 m)

Leaves: 6 to 12 inches (15 to 30 cm) long; 5 to 9 oval leaflets with toothed edges; dark green on top and paler green underneath

Seeds: Dry, flat samaras 1 to 2 inches (2.5 to 5 cm) long with 1 wing

North American Range: Central and eastern Canada and United States

Habitat: Swamps, bottomlands, and open fields

WHITE ASH *(FRAXINUS AMERICANA)*

The white ash has a straight trunk and dense branches. Purple flowers bloom in April and May before the leaves appear. The flowers grow in clusters and do not have petals. Male and female flowers grow on separate trees. In fall, female flowers give way to clusters of samaras. The clusters are six to eight inches (15 to 20 cm) long and droop from the tree. The leaves turn yellow and then purple in fall.

HOW TO SPOT

Height: 50 to 120 feet (15 to 37 m)

Leaves: 8 to 12 inches (20 to 30 cm) long with 5 to 9 oval leaflets; dark green on top and light green underneath

Seeds: Flat, dry samaras 1 to 3 inches (2.5 to 8 cm) long

North American Range: Eastern North America and Mexico

Habitat: Moist areas including river bottoms and well-drained upland woods

FUN FACT

The juice from the leaves of the white ash helps relieve itching and swelling from mosquito bites.

BIGLEAF MAPLE

(ACER MACROPHYLLUM)

Bigleaf maples are the tallest maples in North America. They have reddish-brown bark with deep furrows. In spring, clusters of small yellowish-green flowers appear. The tree's giant leaves are almost as long as they are wide. The samaras develop in summer and mature in fall. The leaves turn yellow or orange before they drop.

HOW TO SPOT

Height: 50 to 160 feet (15 to 49 m)

Leaves: 8 to 12 inches (20 to 30 cm) wide with 3 to 5 lobes; shiny green

Seeds: Samaras up to 2 inches (5 cm) long; wings form a V shape

North American Range: Pacific Northwest and the foothills of the Cascade Range and Coast Mountains

Habitat: Moist areas in woods including floodplains and along streams

THE BIGLEAF ECOSYSTEM

In moist climates, many other plants grow on the trunks and branches of the bigleaf maple. These include mosses, lichens, and ferns. These plants do not hurt the tree. When they die and decay, they create soil in the deep furrows of the bark. This soil provides moisture and nutrients for other plants and animals.

BOXELDER *(ACER NEGUNDO)*

The boxelder is a fast-growing tree. Its fast growth makes its wood weak and brittle. Because of this, boxelder trees are easily damaged by wind and storms. From March through May, yellowish-green flowers appear with the tree's leaves. The flowers develop into samaras from August through October. Boxelder trees also produce sap that contains a lot of sugar. People use the sap to make syrup. People sometimes call this syrup mountain molasses.

Samaras

HOW TO SPOT

Height: 30 to 50 feet (9 to 15 m)

Leaves: Bright green leaves; 3 leaflets 2 to 4 inches (5 to 10 cm) long with toothed edges

Seeds: Samaras about 1 to 2 inches (2.5 to 5 cm) long

North American Range: Across North America from east to west, from Alberta, Canada, to Mexico

Habitat: Wet soils including bottomlands, floodplains, and along lakes and streams

GOLDEN RAINTREE

(KOELREUTERIA PANICULATA)

The golden raintree is native to China, Japan, and Korea. It was first brought to North America in 1763. Today it is an invasive species in the United States. The golden raintree is named for its flowers. In June and July, large clusters of small yellow flowers bloom. When the flowers fall, they resemble golden rain. They form a yellow carpet under the tree. The leaves turn yellow in fall.

HOW TO SPOT

Height: 30 to 40 feet (9 to 12 m)

Leaves: Up to 18 inches (46 cm) long; 7 to 17 leaflets with toothed edges

Seeds: Pink papery capsules with small black seeds inside

North American Range: Southern United States

Habitat: Areas with well-drained soil

OHIO BUCKEYE *(AESCULUS GLABRA)*

The Ohio buckeye has low branches that droop toward the ground and then sweep back up. Greenish-yellow flowers bloom in April or May. Each flower has four petals. The flowers grow in clusters on the ends of the branches. All parts of the Ohio buckeye are poisonous to people if eaten, including the nuts. However, people often use the nuts for making crafts. The twigs and leaves give off an unpleasant smell if crushed. The leaves turn bright orange and yellow in fall.

HOW TO SPOT

Height: 60 to 70 feet (18 to 21 m)

Leaves: Compound leaves with 5 oval leaflets 3 to 6 inches (8 to 15 cm) long with toothed edges; green on top and lighter underneath

Seeds: Spiny, golden-brown capsules containing 1 to 3 large nuts

North American Range: Ontario, Canada, and the eastern half of the United States

Habitat: Moist soils on floodplains and bottomlands, sometimes found along roadsides and fences

Seed

FUN FACT

The Ohio buckeye's name comes from its seeds. These shiny brown nuts with a light patch resemble the eye of a deer. A male deer is called a buck.

PAPERBARK MAPLE *(ACER GRISEUM)*

The paperbark maple is native to China. It often grows more than one trunk. When the tree is about two years old, the dark brown outer layer of bark peels back and curls. This bark stays attached to the trunk instead of falling to the ground. It reveals lighter brown bark underneath. The paperbark maple is one of the last maple trees to develop fall leaf colors. The leaves may turn shades of red, orange, or pink. The leaves remain on the tree into winter.

HOW TO SPOT

Height: 20 to 30 feet (6 to 9 m)

Leaves: Compound leaves with 3 leaflets 3 to 6 inches (8 to 15 cm) long; dark green to bluish green on top and silver underneath

Seeds: Brown or copper samaras 1 to 3 inches (2.5 to 8 cm) long

North American Range: Pacific Northwest

Habitat: Areas with moist, well-drained soil

RED MAPLE *(ACER RUBRUM)*

The red maple is named for the red color of its flowers, fruits, twigs, and especially its fall leaves. Female flowers are redder than male flowers. The flowers grow in drooping clusters. The fruits mature in spring. In fall the red maple is one of the first trees to change color. The leaves may be red, yellow, or orange. The tree's sap contains a lot of sugar. It is used to make maple syrup.

HOW TO SPOT

Height: 40 to 70 feet (12 to 21 m); may grow up to 120 feet (37 m)

Leaves: 2 to 6 inches (5 to 15 cm) long with 3 to 5 lobes and toothed edges

Seeds: Red to brown samaras 1 to 2 inches (2.5 to 5 cm) long; wings form a V shape

North American Range: Eastern North America

Habitat: Forests, ridges, and swamps

SILVER MAPLE *(ACER SACCHARINUM)*

The silver maple is a large tree with a short trunk. It has long, curving branches. The silver maple is the first maple tree to bloom in North America. As early as February, flowers start to grow before the leaves develop. The flowers begin as red buds that are easy to see in winter. When they bloom, they are greenish yellow and grow in clusters. The leaves turn yellow to brown in fall. If the leaves or twigs are crushed, they give off an unpleasant smell.

HOW TO SPOT

Height: 90 to 120 feet (27 to 37 m)

Leaves: 5 lobes that come to a sharp point with 3 to 6 large teeth and some smaller ones; green on top, white or silver underneath

Seeds: Samaras about 2 inches (5 cm) long

North American Range: Eastern United States

Habitat: Moist soil around streams, lakes, swamps, and floodplains

SUGAR MAPLE *(ACER SACCHARUM)*

The branches of the sugar maple emerge in pairs. The sap of the sugar maple has twice as much sugar as that of other maple species. This is the main tree used to produce maple syrup. The sap is collected in late winter and early spring. Rising temperatures help the sap to flow. Small, pale yellow flowers bloom in spring. The winged seeds follow and drop in late summer. In fall the leaves may be bright yellow, orange, or red.

HOW TO SPOT

Height: 60 to 75 feet (18 to 23 m)

Leaves: Dark green leaves with 5 lobes; 3 to 6 inches (8 to 15 cm) long

Seeds: U-shaped, brown samaras about 1 inch (2.5 cm) long

North American Range: Eastern Canada and northeastern United States

Habitat: Areas with well-drained sand

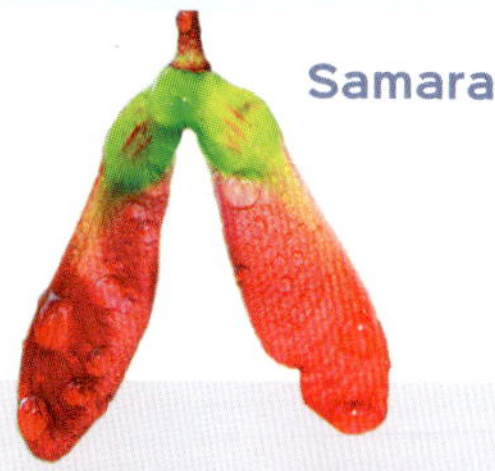

Samara

A SWEET INDUSTRY

It takes about 43 gallons (163 L) of sap to make one gallon (4 L) of maple syrup. One tap in a tree produces eight to ten gallons (30 to 38 L) of sap in a season. Maple syrup production is a large industry in North America. Canada produces more than 70 percent of the world's maple syrup. The rest is produced in the United States.

WESTERN SOAPBERRY

(SAPINDUS DRUMMONDII)

The western soapberry is a small- to medium-sized tree with a round canopy. Yellowish-white flowers bloom in clusters. The flowers develop into fruits that resemble grapes. However, the fruits are poisonous to humans. The fruits mature in September and October. Those that stay on the tree eventually turn black. If the fruits are mashed, they produce a soapy lather. In fall the leaves turn gold.

FUN FACT

American Indians and early European settlers used western soapberry fruits to make soap.

Fruits

HOW TO SPOT

Height: 40 to 50 feet (12 to 15 m)

Leaves: Compound leaves 15 inches (38 cm) long with 8 to 18 leaflets; glossy green on top and fuzzy underneath

Seeds: Yellowish-orange fruits, each containing 1 seed, grow in clusters

North American Range: Southwestern United States and northern Mexico

Habitat: Moist areas along rivers and streams

YELLOW BUCKEYE *(AESCULUS FLAVA)*

The yellow buckeye is one of the first trees to grow leaves in spring. In May, tube-shaped clusters of creamy yellow flowers grow upright on branches. They are up to six inches (15 cm) tall. They often rise above the leaves all over the tree. The fruits mature in September and October. The seeds contain a toxin that can be deadly to animals. Some people carry the seeds around as good luck charms. The leaves of the yellow buckeye turn bright orange during fall.

HOW TO SPOT

Height: 60 to 90 feet (18 to 27 m)

Leaves: Compound, made up of 5 to 7 dark green leaflets 3 to 7 inches (8 to 18 cm) long with toothed edges

Seeds: Round and leathery fruits 2 to 3 inches (5 to 8 cm) long; each contains 1 to 3 shiny brown seeds

North American Range: Southeastern United States, especially in the southern Appalachian and Great Smoky Mountains

Habitat: Along rivers and streams, and in moist forests, coves, and northern slopes

BALSAM POPLAR

(POPULUS BALSAMIFERA)

The balsam poplar is a large tree with branches that grow upright. The leaves give off a sweet smell. The bark is smooth and light gray on younger trees. Furrows form in the bark as the tree grows older. Flowers begin to form when the tree is about eight to ten years old. The flowers produce a large number of seeds almost every year. In fall the tree's leaves turn yellow.

HOW TO SPOT

Height: 30 to 100 feet (9 to 30 m)

Leaves: 2 to 4.5 inches (5 to 11 cm) long with toothed edges; shiny dark green on top and silver or brown underneath

Seeds: Each seed is attached to a tuft of long, silky hair

North American Range: From Canada to the northern United States

Habitat: Floodplains, creek banks, lakeshores, swamps, and hillsides

BIGTOOTH ASPEN

(POPULUS GRANDIDENTATA)

The bigtooth aspen is a very fast-growing tree. It is one of the first trees to grow in areas that have been burned. Its slender branches create a narrow, round canopy. The flowers appear in early spring. They grow on fuzzy catkins. The leaves emerge later in spring, at about the same time as the fruits ripen. The seeds are small and light. Wind carries them long distances. The leaves turn yellow in fall.

HOW TO SPOT

Height: 60 to 80 feet (18 to 24 m)

Leaves: Dark green, egg-shaped leaves; 3 to 4 inches (8 to 10 cm) long; 5 to 15 large, curved teeth on each side of the leaf and a short, pointed tip

Seeds: Small capsules contain tiny seeds with silky hairs

North American Range: Southeastern Canada and north-central and northeastern United States

Habitat: Moist soils near streams

BLACK WILLOW *(SALIX NIGRA)*

The black willow tree is native to the United States. It is a fast-growing tree. Several trunks will often grow at different angles from one root. Its bark is dark brown to black with deep furrows and shaggy scales. Male and female flowers grow on separate trees. Fruits grow on the female trees only. When ready, the fruit capsules open to release seeds. When the seeds fall, wind and water catch the long, silky hairs and carry away the seeds. The leaves turn yellowish green in fall.

HOW TO SPOT

Height: 30 to 140 feet (9 to 43 m)

Leaves: Green; up to 6 inches (15 cm) long; narrow with small teeth along the edges

Seeds: Hanging clusters of dry light brown capsules hold tiny green seeds attached to silky hairs

North American Range: Eastern United States and parts of Canada and Mexico

Habitat: Moist to wet soils such as floodplains, riverbanks, swamps, and marshes

NATURAL MEDICINE

Willow trees have been used for healing purposes for centuries. The ancient Greeks used willow bark to make tea to treat stiff joints. Willow bark has also been used to reduce fevers. Some people still use willow bark instead of aspirin to relieve pain.

EASTERN COTTONWOOD

(POPULUS DELTOIDES)

The eastern cottonwood is a large, fast-growing tree. Some trees may grow more than six feet (1.8 m) each year. The tree has a large trunk that often splits into thick, sturdy branches. The branches grow upright and droop at the tips. Flowers grow in clusters. They do not have petals and may be red, gold, or green. The tree's leaves turn yellow in fall. In the late spring and early summer, its seed capsules open. The seeds appear as cotton-like clusters.

FUN FACT

Cottonwood trees are the fastest-growing native trees in North America.

Seeds

HOW TO SPOT

Height: 75 to 100 feet (23 to 30 m)

Leaves: Smooth, glossy, paper-like leaves 3 to 6 inches (8 to 15 cm) long; light to medium green; triangular with curved teeth

Seeds: Green egg-shaped capsules containing many seeds with silky white hairs

North American Range: Southern Canada; southwestern, central, and eastern United States; and northern Mexico

Habitat: Along streams, riverbanks, and bottomlands

QUAKING ASPEN

(POPULUS TREMULOIDES)

The quaking aspen tree reproduces mostly through its roots. Quaking aspens grow in large, dense groups called stands. The trees in each stand are connected by the same root system. New trunks grow up from the roots as they spread underground. The leaves are attached to the branches by long, flat stalks. The leaves flutter or quake in even a light breeze, giving the tree its name. The leaves turn yellow in fall.

Because they share roots, all the quaking aspens in a stand change color at the same time.

HOW TO SPOT

Height: 40 to 100 feet (12 to 30 m)

Leaves: Flat leaves about 1 to 3 inches (2.5 to 8 cm) long with toothed edges and long stalks

Seeds: Oval fruits about 0.25 inches (6 cm) long containing small seeds, each with a tuft of long, white, silky hair

North American Range: Across North America except in the Southeast

Habitat: Moist soils along forest edges

WEEPING WILLOW *(SALIX BABYLONICA)*

The weeping willow is native to northern China. It has a short trunk with long, drooping branches and long, thin leaves. Some of the longer branches may reach the ground. Weeping willows can grow three feet (1 m) or more each year. Because of their fast growth, the wood is weak and can crack or break easily. Weeping willow leaves turn greenish yellow in fall.

HOW TO SPOT

Height: 30 to 50 feet (9 to 15 m)

Leaves: Broad, flat leaves 3 to 6 inches (8 to 15 cm) long with toothed edges; green on top and gray underneath

Seeds: Dry green to brown capsules about 1 inch (2.5 cm) long with cotton-like seeds

North American Range: From southeastern Canada to Georgia and in some western states

Habitat: Near bodies of water

FUN FACT

Weeping willows are easy to grow from stems. A cut stem placed in soil about six inches (15 cm) deep can develop roots and grow into a tree.

BLACK TUPELO *(NYSSA SYLVATICA)*

The black tupelo has a thick trunk with many branches. The tree's bark is gray to black and has deep furrows that create rectangular or square ridges. The small greenish-yellow flowers grow in clusters in April and May. Fruits appear from late summer to fall. The fruits grow in clusters of two to three. They ripen in late September and early October. The fruits are edible but taste sour. In fall the leaves turn many shades of yellow, orange, red, and purple.

HOW TO SPOT

Height: 40 to 100 feet (12 to 30 m)

Leaves: Oval or egg-shaped leaves 3 to 6 inches (8 to 15 cm) long; dark green on top and paler underneath; some leaves have teeth

Seeds: Bluish-black round or oval fruits less than 1 inch (2.5 cm) long; inside are small, ribbed seeds

North American Range: Eastern North America and Mexico

Habitat: Moist, well-drained soils in forests, meadows, fields, and swamps and along streams, lakes, and rivers

WATER TUPELO *(NYSSA AQUATICA)*

The water tupelo has a long, straight trunk. The base of the trunk is swollen and flares outward. This feature helps the tree remain stable in wet soil. Flowers and leaves appear at the same time in spring. Male and female flowers grow on separate trees. The female flowers grow alone on long stalks. The male flowers grow in round clusters. Fruits become black as they ripen in September. The leaves turn yellow in fall.

HOW TO SPOT

Height: 60 to 100 feet (18 to 30 m)

Leaves: Glossy, egg-shaped, dark green leaves 4 to 8 inches (10 to 20 cm) long; paler and fuzzy underneath

Seeds: Dark purple fruits about 1 inch (2.5 cm) long with tough skin; each contains 1 flat, ridged seed

North American Range: Southeastern United States along the coast and up the southern Mississippi River

Habitat: Swamps and floodplains

AMERICAN HORNBEAM

(CARPINUS CAROLINIANA)

The American hornbeam is a small, slow-growing tree. It may have one or more trunks. The tree is also called musclewood. This name comes from the appearance of the trunk and larger branches. The bumps underneath the bark look similar to human muscles. The flowers are yellowish green and bloom in spring. The fruits form clusters of winged seeds. The leaves turn yellow, orange, or red in fall.

HOW TO SPOT

Height: 15 to 25 feet (5 to 8 m)

Leaves: 2.5 to 5 inches (6 to 13 cm) long with toothed edges; green on top and paler underneath

Seeds: Small nutlets about 0.4 inches (1 cm) long; each is attached to a scale with 3 lobes

North American Range: Eastern Canada and United States

Habitat: Forests and the banks of streams and rivers

EASTERN HOPHORNBEAM

(OSTRYA VIRGINIANA)

The eastern hophornbeam is a small tree with long, thin branches. The branches often droop at the ends. Flowers bloom in April and May before the leaves appear. Male and female flowers grow in catkins on the same tree. The male flowers are reddish brown. The female flowers develop into pods that hang at the ends of the branches. Each pod looks like a small inflated pouch. The leaves of the eastern hophornbeam turn yellow in fall. They often drop earlier than those of other trees. The male flowers last throughout winter.

HOW TO SPOT

Height: 20 to 40 feet (6 to 12 m)

Leaves: 2 to 5 inches (5 to 13 cm) long with toothed edges and a pointed tip; dark green on top and paler and hairy underneath

Seeds: Drooping clusters of dried, leafy pods that contain 1 hard nutlet

North American Range: Eastern half of Canada and United States and parts of southern Mexico

Habitat: Dry, rocky forests and slopes

Flowers

GRAY BIRCH *(BETULA POPULIFOLIA)*

Gray birch is a fast-growing tree. It grows about two feet (0.6 m) each year. However, it lives only about 20 years. It has short, thin branches. They can almost touch the ground. One tree often has several trunks that lean to the side. Yellow flowers bloom between April and May. The tree has chalky white bark that does not peel. Black triangle-shaped patches show where branches were once attached to the trunk. The leaves turn yellow in fall.

HOW TO SPOT

Height: 20 to 40 feet (6 to 12 m)

Leaves: Dark green, shiny, triangular leaves 2 to 3 inches (5 to 8 cm) long with a long point and toothed edges

Seeds: Clusters of samaras 2 to 3 inches (5 to 8 cm) long located at the ends of branches

North American Range: Nova Scotia, Canada, and northeastern United States

Habitat: Roadsides, open areas, woodland edges, and moist, well-drained soil near streams, ponds, lakes, and swamps

PAPER BIRCH *(BETULA PAPYRIFERA)*

The paper birch tree is known for its unusual white bark. Its bark develops in layers that resemble paper. The outer layers are loose. As the tree grows older, the bark curls and peels back. Underneath is a light-pink-colored bark. The tree may also have dark triangular markings. These are the places where branches have died and fallen off. The tree's flowers grow in catkins. Winter winds easily blow the seeds across the snow to scatter them. The leaves turn yellow in fall.

HOW TO SPOT

Height: 50 to 70 feet (15 to 21 m)

Leaves: Oval or triangular leaves 2 to 4 inches (5 to 10 cm) long with toothed edges

Seeds: Tiny brown seeds less than 0.1 inches (0.25 cm) long

North American Range: Canada and the northwestern United States including Alaska

Habitat: Forests and areas disturbed by logging or fires

FUN FACT

The bark of the paper birch is water resistant. American Indians and early European fur trappers used it to make canoes.

RIVER BIRCH *(BETULA NIGRA)*

The river birch is a fast-growing tree. Unlike other birch trees, the bark of the river birch is dark instead of white. The bark becomes rougher and darker as the tree grows older. It peels away throughout the year. Male and female flowers form on the same tree. The male flowers grow in clusters at the ends of twigs. Similar to those of other birch trees, the flowers form in fall and stay on the twigs all winter. Female flowers do not bloom until spring. The leaves of the river birch turn yellow or brown in fall.

HOW TO SPOT

Height: 50 to 90 feet (15 to 27 m)

Leaves: Wide leaf bases create a triangle shape; shiny and green on top and paler underneath with toothed edges

Seeds: Reddish-brown cone-like structures 1 inch (2.5 cm) long containing winged seeds

North American Range: Eastern United States

Habitat: Along rivers and streams, floodplains, and swamps

SWEET BIRCH *(BETULA LENTA)*

The sweet birch tree gets its name from its sweet scent. Its crushed stems and broken twigs smell similar to wintergreen. Small green flowers mature in early spring. The male flowers grow in drooping clusters. Female flowers are smaller and grow upright. They develop into small cones one to 1.5 inches (2.5 to 4 cm) long. The cones contain many tiny seeds that ripen in fall. Wind blows the seeds to new areas. The leaves turn golden yellow in fall.

HOW TO SPOT

Height: 60 to 70 feet (18 to 21 m)

Leaves: Light green and 2 to 6 inches (5 to 15 cm) long with toothed edges

Seeds: Cones 1 to 1.5 inches (2.5 to 4 cm) long hold small, 2-winged nutlets

North American Range: Eastern North America from Quebec, Canada, to the US state of Georgia

Habitat: Forests, mountains, and slopes

FUN FACT

Sweet birch oil has a cooling feeling when applied to the skin. People sometimes use it to relieve sore muscles.

WHITE ALDER *(ALNUS RHOMBIFOLIA)*

The white alder is a fast-growing tree. It grows about three feet (1 m) per year. The flowers are green or yellow. They grow in catkins. The female flowers develop into fruits that look like small cones. Throughout winter, male catkins hang from the branches. The cones may stay on the tree for up to one year. White alder trees have scaly light gray bark. Most of their leaves don't change color in fall before dropping.

HOW TO SPOT

Height: 50 to 100 feet (15 to 30 m) or taller

Leaves: Flat, egg-shaped leaves with toothed edges; dark green and glossy on top and lighter green underneath

Seeds: Fruits are about 0.75 inches (2 cm) long and look similar to small brown pine cones

North American Range: Cascade Range and Sierra Nevada in the western United States

Habitat: Along streams and rivers and on rocky slopes

Fruits

YELLOW BIRCH

(BETULA ALLEGHANIENSIS)

The yellow birch gets its name from the color of its bark. The bark on young stems, branches, and trunks is golden yellow. It peels in thin, curly strips. As the tree grows older, the bark appears shredded. When the tree is about one foot (0.3 m) wide, the curls wear away. The bark appears brown and scaly. Small yellow, green, or brown flowers appear on branches just before the leaves in spring. The leaves turn bright yellow in fall.

HOW TO SPOT

Height: 70 to 80 feet (21 to 24 m)

Leaves: Toothed, oval leaves 2.5 to 4 inches (6 to 10 cm) long with a pointed tip; dark green on top and lighter underneath

Seeds: 1.5-inch (4 cm) hairy cones; each contains nutlets with 2 wings

North American Range: From eastern Canada to the Great Lakes, and from the Appalachian Mountains to Georgia

Habitat: Moist woodlands

AMERICAN BASSWOOD

(TILIA AMERICANA)

The American basswood tree is a main nectar source for honeybees. Its yellow flowers bloom in late May or June. These fragrant flowers attract large numbers of honeybees. People can sometimes hear their buzzing from several feet away. The flowers grow underneath a large leaf-like structure called a wing. In summer and fall, small nutlets develop under each wing. When ripe, the nutlets and wings fall. The wind helps carry the nutlets to new locations.

HOW TO SPOT

Height: 60 to 80 feet (18 to 24 m)

Leaves: Large heart-shaped leaves with toothed edges; dark green on top and gray underneath

Seeds: Clusters of hard nutlets on a stem attached to the center of a leaf-like structure

North American Range: Northwestern North America, southeastern Canada, and the eastern United States

Habitat: Moist upland woods, slopes, and ravines

SOURWOOD *(OXYDENDRUM ARBOREUM)*

The sourwood tree is named for the sour taste of its leaves. Its white flowers are fragrant. The flowers appear in June and July after the leaves are fully grown. They are waxy and bell shaped. After the flowers drop, the long stems resemble fingers. In early fall, the leaves turn bright red. The seed capsules ripen in September and October, turning silvery gray. They remain on the tree after the leaves have fallen.

HOW TO SPOT

Height: 20 to 30 feet (6 to 9 m)

Leaves: Glossy green oval leaves; 3 to 6 inches (8 to 15 cm) long with toothed edges

Seeds: Dry brown seed capsules about 0.5 inches (1.3 cm) long with 5 compartments

North American Range: Eastern and southern United States

Habitat: Woodlands, ravines, clearings, and well-drained slopes and hills

FUN FACT

Sourwood honey is produced from the flowers' pollen. It has a natural flavor of anise.

AMERICAN PERSIMMON

(DIOSPYROS VIRGINIANA)

The American persimmon tree is a slow-growing tree with edible fruits. Its flowers are small and fragrant. They are white to greenish yellow and bloom from May to June. Male flowers appear in small clusters. Female flowers are bell shaped and grow alone. Fruits appear on trees with female flowers from September to December. The fruits are very sweet when ripe. In fall the tree's leaves turn yellow to reddish purple.

Ripe fruits

HOW TO SPOT

Height: 30 to 80 feet (9 to 24 m)

Leaves: Egg-shaped leaves are 2 to 6 inches (5 to 15 cm) long; dark green on top and paler with dark veins and hairs underneath

Seeds: Edible yellow to orange fruits are about 1 to 1.5 inches (2.5 to 4 cm) long and contain flat seeds

North American Range: Central and eastern United States, as far north as Connecticut

Habitat: Rocky or dry open woods, unused fields, clearings, and roadsides

SWEETGUM *(LIQUIDAMBAR STYRACIFLUA)*

The sweetgum tree gets its name from its sweet-smelling sap. The sap oozes out when the tree has a wound, such as a scrape. The leaves also give off a sweet smell if crushed. Small branches and twigs often have ridges growing on the sides. The flowers grow in clusters, but they can be difficult to see. They are yellowish green and grow near the top of the tree. They develop into prickly seed balls. In fall the leaves turn a mixture of orange, red, yellow, and purple.

HOW TO SPOT

Height: 60 to 100 feet (18 to 30 m)

Leaves: Glossy, star-shaped leaves with 5 to 7 pointed lobes and toothed edges

Seeds: Spiny, round balls containing winged seeds

North American Range: Eastern United States and Mexico

Habitat: In valleys and along streams

Seed ball

GINKGO *(GINKGO BILOBA)*

The ginkgo tree is native to eastern China. In North America it is often planted in cities. Male trees produce pollen, and female trees bear seeds. The seeds give off a very unpleasant smell. For this reason people often plant only the male trees. In fall the leaves turn bright yellow and gold. Ginkgo trees often drop most of their leaves in a short time, sometimes overnight. The leaves may look like a yellow carpet under the tree.

FUN FACT

Scientists call the ginkgo tree a living fossil because it has existed for more than 200 million years and changed very little during that time.

HOW TO SPOT

Height: 50 to 80 feet (15 to 24 m)

Leaves: Fan-shaped leaves 2 to 3 inches (5 to 8 cm) long; notched at the tip

Seeds: Shaped similar to a plum, with a tan or orange fleshy covering

North American Range: Along the Saint Lawrence River in Canada and midwestern and eastern United States

Habitat: Planted in urban areas and grows best in sandy, moist soil

SASSAFRAS *(SASSAFRAS ALBIDUM)*

The sassafras tree often has more than one trunk. It also has many short, horizontal branches. Clusters of small yellowish-green flowers appear in spring. These develop into clusters of fruits in late summer. Many parts of the sassafras tree give off a scent. The flowers are fragrant. The bark of a young tree gives off a spicy smell. The leaves are fragrant when crushed. In fall the leaves can turn shades of orange, red, yellow, pink, and purple.

HOW TO SPOT

Height: 30 to 60 feet (9 to 18 m)

Leaves: 4 to 6 inches (10 to 15 cm) long; may be oval, mitten shaped, or have 3 lobes; bright green on top and paler or white underneath

Seeds: Round dark blue fruits 0.5 to 1 inch (1.3 to 2.5 cm) long; contain a single seed

North American Range: Southern Ontario, Canada, and eastern United States

Habitat: Woodlands, roadsides, empty fields, and along fences

FUN FACT

Root beer used to be flavored from the bark of sassafras roots.

CHINABERRY *(MELIA AZEDARACH)*

The chinaberry tree is native to Asia. In the late 1700s, it was introduced to the United States as an ornamental tree. Today chinaberry trees are often considered invasive. They adapt well to many environments and crowd out native plants. One tree often has several smaller trunks. The flowers are small and star shaped. They are usually pink to lavender and give off a fragrant chocolate scent.

HOW TO SPOT

Height: 30 to 50 feet (9 to 15 m)

Leaves: 1 to 2 feet (0.3 to 0.6 m) long and 9 to 16 inches (23 to 41 cm) wide; dark green color on top and lighter green underneath

Seeds: Clusters of round yellow to tan berries containing 1 to 6 seeds

North American Range: Southeastern United States

Habitat: Along roadsides and in forest openings and thickets

Berries

EMPRESS *(PAULOWNIA TOMENTOSA)*

The empress tree is native to China. It was introduced to the United States in about 1840. Today it is considered an invasive species. The empress tree grows 15 feet (5 m) each year and is one of the fastest-growing trees in the world. Its canopy produces a lot of shade. This makes it difficult for other plants to grow underneath it. The flowers are light purple to pink with dark spots and yellow stripes. They bloom before the leaves emerge and grow in long clusters that smell like vanilla.

FUN FACT

The empress tree was named in honor of Princess Anna Pavlovna of Russia. She lived from the late 1700s to the mid-1800s.

HOW TO SPOT

Height: 30 to 50 feet (9 to 15 m)

Leaves: Oval or heart shaped and 5 to 12 inches (13 to 30 cm) long; dark green with some hairs on top and paler underneath

Seeds: Brown egg-shaped capsules are 1 to 1.5 inches (2.5 to 4 cm) long, containing up to 2,000 small, winged seeds

North American Range: Eastern United States

Habitat: Open areas in forests where trees have been removed

ALPINE LARCH *(LARIX LYALLII)*

The alpine larch has branches that grow horizontally from the trunk. The branches are often twisted. Sometimes they hang down loosely from the tree. However, they stay connected to the tree even if they die. Young twigs are covered with a dense, fuzzy coating ranging in color from white to yellow. Alpine larches are deciduous conifers. They begin producing cones when they are 100 years old. The seeds mature in September. The needles turn golden yellow in fall.

HOW TO SPOT

Height: Up to 82 feet (25 m)

Leaves: Light bluish-green needles 2.5 to 3.5 inches (6 to 9 cm) long; growing in clusters of 30 to 40

Seeds: Yellow to purple cones 1 to 2 inches (2.5 to 5 cm) long; each contains winged seeds

North American Range: Canadian provinces of Alberta and British Columbia and US states of Washington, Idaho, and Montana

Habitat: Cold, snowy, and moist mountain regions of the northern Rocky Mountains and northern Cascade Range

DECIDUOUS CONIFERS

Most trees are deciduous or coniferous. Deciduous trees drop their leaves every year. Coniferous trees produce cones and have needles or scales. Coniferous trees usually keep their needles or scales through winter. Deciduous conifers produce cones and have needles. But their needles often change color, and they drop each year.

DAWN REDWOOD

(METASEQUOIA GLYPTOSTROBOIDES)

The dawn redwood is the smallest of the redwood trees. It is a fast-growing tree. It can grow four feet (1.2 m) each year. The branches droop as the tree grows older. The leaves are needles. They are light green when they first grow. During summer they turn deep green. In fall they become reddish brown. All the needles drop in fall.

HOW TO SPOT

Height: 62 to 100 feet (19 to 30 m)

Leaves: Soft, feathery needles less than 1 inch (2.5 cm) long; closely packed together

Seeds: Dark brown cones hold seeds; cones are up to 1 inch (2.5 cm) long with 14 to 28 scales

North American Range: Eastern and southeastern United States

Habitat: Low-lying areas near rivers and streams

AN AMAZING DISCOVERY

Fossil records show that dawn redwoods once thrived in North America. But for many years scientists thought these trees were extinct. In 1944 dawn redwoods were rediscovered by a Chinese forester. About 1,000 dawn redwoods grew in southeastern China. Scientists collected seeds from these trees and planted them around the world to help the dawn redwood survive.

GOLDEN LARCH

(PSEUDOLARIX AMABILIS)

The golden larch is native to southeastern China. Golden larches have horizontal branches with smaller branches that droop. Male and female cones grow on the same tree. Male cones grow at the ends of the branches. They usually appear in groups of 10 to 25. Seeds develop in the female cones. These cones have soft, fragile scales. They drop and fall apart when the seeds ripen. During fall the leaves turn bright gold, yellow, or orange. They drop before winter.

HOW TO SPOT

Height: 40 to 70 feet (12 to 21 m)

Leaves: Soft, flat needles about 2 inches (5 cm) long; light green on top and bluish green underneath

Seeds: Reddish-brown cones about 3 inches (8 cm) long; cones contain white, oval-winged seeds

North American Range: Pacific Northwest

Habitat: Moist, well-drained soil

POND CYPRESS

(TAXODIUM DISTICHUM VAR. IMBRICARIUM)

The pond cypress tree has a straight trunk that grows thicker toward the base. This provides support for the tree in its wet habitat. The roots form bumpy cone shapes that stick up from the ground. These exposed roots are called knees. The knees are about one foot (0.3 m) tall. The branches are often covered in Spanish moss. The leaves turn light brown to bright orange before dropping in fall. Also in fall the cones mature and release the seeds.

HOW TO SPOT

Height: 30 to 70 feet (9 to 21 m)

Leaves: Rounded, scale-like leaves up to 0.4 inches (1 cm) long grow upright

Seeds: Brown cones are about 0.5 to 1 inch (1.3 to 2.5 cm) long and contain winged seeds

North American Range: Gulf Coast region of the southern United States

Habitat: Swamps and edges of streams, lakes, and ponds

GLOSSARY

bottomland
Low-lying land along a river or stream, often prone to flooding.

bristle
A short, stiff hair or spine found on the surface of some leaves.

bur
A rough, prickly covering or seed casing.

canopy
The top layer of leaves and branches on a tree.

catkin
A slim, cylindrical flower cluster, usually hanging or drooping.

cove
A small, sheltered area often surrounded by hills or cliffs.

edible
Safe for people to eat.

floodplain
Flat or nearly flat land next to a river or stream that experiences occasional flooding.

fragrant
Pleasant smelling.

furrow
A shallow groove or trench in the bark of a tree.

husk
The dry outer covering of some fruits or seeds.

lobe
A rounded or pointed projection on a leaf.

mature
Fully developed and able to reproduce.

nutlet
A small nut or nut-like seed.

ornamental
For decoration or beauty.

pagoda
A tower in eastern Asia with several roofs that curve upward.

plate
A large, flat section or layer of bark.

ravine
A deep, narrow valley with steep sides.

samara
A type of dry fruit with a flattened wing-like structure that allows it to be carried by the wind.

tooth
A small, pointed projection along the edge of a leaf, often giving it a jagged appearance.

TO LEARN MORE

FURTHER READINGS

Debbink, Andrea. *Trees*. Abdo, 2021.

Farley, Christin. *The Little Book of North American Trees*. Bushel & Peck, 2023.

Murray, Laura K. *Conifers*. Abdo, 2026.

ONLINE RESOURCES

To learn more about North American deciduous trees, please visit **abdobooklinks.com** or scan this QR code. These links are routinely monitored and updated to provide the most current information available.

PHOTO CREDITS

Cover Photos: Marco de Benedictis/Shutterstock Images, front (top left); Shutterstock Images, front (top right, upper left, upper center, middle left, bottom center, bottom right), back (right); Ken Wolter/Shutterstock Images, front (upper right); Kit Leong/Shutterstock Images, front (middle right); Getty Images, front (bottom left); Doug Gordon/Shutterstock Images, back (left)

Interior Photos: iStockphoto, 1 (left), 1 (right), 4 (bottom right), 5 (top right), 5 (bottom left), 9 (left), 15, 16 (top), 24 (right), 25 (top), 26 (right), 27 (right), 30 (top), 39 (left), 41 (left), 43 (top), 44 (bottom), 50, 53, 56 (right), 72 (bottom), 76 (left), 77 (left), 89 (right), 92 (right), 96 (right), 100 (bottom), 102 (left); Andrew Julian Photography/Shutterstock Images, 4 (bottom left), 36 (right), 88 (right); Melinda Fawver/Shutterstock Images, 4–5, 57, 61, 63 (left), 76 (right); Shutterstock Images, 5 (top left), 5 (bottom right), 9 (right), 11 (right), 13 (right), 14 (right), 16 (bottom), 18 (right), 20 (right), 21 (left), 22, 23 (left), 27 (left), 28, 29, 31, 32, 34, 35 (bottom), 37 (right), 38, 39 (right), 41 (right), 42, 47 (left), 47 (right), 48 (top), 55 (bottom), 56 (left), 58 (left), 60, 62 (top), 64, 65 (left), 66 (left), 68 (bottom), 69, 70 (left), 71 (right), 72 (top), 73 (top), 74 (left), 74 (right), 75, 84 (left), 87 (left), 91 (left), 94 (right), 95 (left), 96 (left), 97 (right), 98 (bottom), 100 (top), 101 (top), 101 (bottom), 102 (right), 103 (right), 104, 112 (left); John Ruberry/Shutterstock Images, 6, 82; Kit Leong/Shutterstock Images, 6–7, 10, 83 (left); Merrimon Crawford/Shutterstock Images, 7, 83 (right); Peter Turner Photography/Shutterstock Images, 8, 12 (top), 37 (left), 51 (top), 52 (right), 55 (top), 73 (bottom), 79, 86, 105, 106, 107 (left); Sahara Frost/Shutterstock Images, 11 (left); Dina Rogatnykh/Shutterstock Images, 12 (bottom); Esin Deniz/Shutterstock Images, 13 (left); Benjamin Ryan Humphrey/Shutterstock Images, 14 (left); Ihor Hvozdetskyi/Shutterstock Images, 17; Khairil Azhar Junos/Shutterstock Images, 18 (left); Wolf Vuk/Shutterstock Images, 19; Peter Jousiffe/Science Source, 20 (left); Tatiana Kuklina/Shutterstock Images, 21 (right); Irina Borsuchenko/Shutterstock Images, 23 (right); Przemyslaw Muszynski/Shutterstock Images, 24 (left); Den Grady/Shutterstock Images, 25 (bottom); Ruth Swan/Shutterstock Images, 26 (left); Orest Lyzhechka/Shutterstock

Images, 30 (bottom); John A. Anderson/Shutterstock Images, 33; Igor Krasilov/Shutterstock Images, 35 (top); DEA/C. Sappa/ De Agostini/Getty Images, 36 (left); piemags/Nature/Alamy, 40 (left), 46, 48 (bottom), 78 (right); Juan Cruzado Cortés/ iNaturalist, 40 (right); Martin Fowler/Shutterstock Images, 43 (bottom); Erika J. Mitchell/ Shutterstock Images, 44 (top); Naohisa Goto/Shutterstock Images, 45; Missouri State Parks, 49 (top); Eric Hunt/ Wikimedia Commons, 49 (bottom); Ole Schoener/ Shutterstock Images, 51 (bottom); Gaga Mumladze/ Shutterstock Images, 52 (left); Tracy Immordino/Shutterstock Images, 54 (top); E. R. Degginger/ Science Source, 54 (bottom); Norm Lane/Shutterstock Images, 58 (right); Shanze Yoell/ iNaturalist, 59 (bottom); Ross Gordon Henry/Shutterstock Images, 59 (top); Rafael Santos Rodriguez/Shutterstock Images, 62 (bottom); Jovana Pantovic/ Shutterstock Images, 63 (right); Jared Quentin/Shutterstock Images, 65 (right); Norman Pogson/Alamy, 66 (right); Dorling Kindersley Ltd./Alamy, 67; Mary Anne Campbell/ Shutterstock Images, 68 (top); Charlie Hawkshaw/Shutterstock Images, 70 (right); Antoniya Kadiyska/Shutterstock Images, 71 (left), 99 (left); Malachi Jacobs/ Shutterstock Images, 77 (right); Cray McDaniel/Shutterstock Images, 78 (left); Peter Himmelhuber/Zoonar GmbH/ Alamy, 80 (left); Henrik Larsson/ Shutterstock Images, 80 (right); Doug Gordon/Shutterstock Images, 81 (left); Michael Gadomski/Alamy, 81 (right), 90; Kristi Blokhin/Shutterstock Images, 84 (right); Daniel Sztork/ Shutterstock Images, 85; Laura Clark/iNaturalist, 87 (right); Gerry Bishop/Shutterstock Images, 88 (left); Jon Benedictus/ Shutterstock Images, 89 (left); Janet Moore/Shutterstock Images, 91 (right); Jorge Salcedo/ Shutterstock Images, 92 (left); Martin Fowler/Shutterstock Images, 93; George Ostertag/ Alamy, 94 (left); Patrick Frischknecht/imageBROKER.com GmbH & Co. KG/Alamy, 95 (right); Sergey Denisenko/Shutterstock Images, 97 (left); Wiert Nieuman/ Shutterstock Images, 98 (top); Frans Blok/Shutterstock Images, 99 (right); AnnaReinert/Zoonar GmbH/Alamy, 103 (left); Erich Teister-etfoto/Zoonar GmbH/ Alamy, 107 (right), 112 (right)

ABDOBOOKS.COM
Published by Abdo Reference, a division of ABDO, PO Box 398166, Minneapolis, Minnesota 55439.

Printed in China.
052025
092025

Editor: Marley Richmond
Series Designer: Colleen McLaren
Production Designer: Laura Kuchar

LIBRARY OF CONGRESS CONTROL NUMBER: 2024949017
PUBLISHER'S CATALOGING-IN-PUBLICATION DATA
Names: Bell, Samantha S., author.
Title: Deciduous trees / by Samantha S. Bell
Description: Minneapolis, Minnesota: Abdo Reference, 2026 | Series: North American field guides | Includes online resources and index.
Identifiers: ISBN 9781098297671 (lib. bdg.) | ISBN 9798384930198 (ebook)
Subjects: LCSH: Trees--Juvenile literature. | Forest plants--Juvenile literature. | Trees--North America—Juvenile literature. | Reference materials--Juvenile literature.
Classification: DDC 635.977--dc23